Reviews

I love this book. It describes how the author aims to set free the souls of those who have died yet who remain trapped in this world; and the generosity and humility with which she shares her comforting story also helps to release those who stay behind. Beautifully illustrated by stories of people's encounters with the continuing life of those no longer here, it is full of hope and inspiration. The author's profound compassion and wisdom are matched by her skill in understanding the bereaved and troubled people she encounters. Reading it will bring relief and renewed vision to many, as it does to me.

Hazel Marshall — Director *Rock-Bank Transpersonal Centre*

Annabel Chaplin writes with authenticity and compassion how, through the release of earthbound spirits into 'the Light', she has been able to free people suffering from the harmful effects of spirit attachment. She asks that we open ourselves to understanding death not as an ending but as a transition to a greater life beyond. A compelling read, with profound implications for the true nature of reality, and the meaning and purpose of human existence.

Dr Andrew Powell — Psychiatrist and author of *The Ways of the Soul*

In the same classical genre as *Testimony of Light*, this book not only draws our attention to those souls who remain earthbound after death of the body, but also gives us perspective on life itself as a soul having a human experience. Annabel Chaplin has given us a vital key that may help many people experiencing the continuing presence of someone who was close to them before death and is now still 'around' in a demanding way. Unless you happen to be an *Om Seti*, this is not healthy for anyone. Both parties need to continue on their separate paths in line with their soul's remit. Anne Baring's wise and comprehensive Introduction is a gem in its own right.

Sue Minns — Former teacher and trustee *College of Psychic Studies*

⁓✳︎⁓

In our materialistic culture, there is widespread ignorance about the true nature of death, which is why the central message of this evidential book is so important: that death is a transition to a new realm of consciousness. Due to this ignorance, we do not prepare for our final journey, so many people do not realise they have died and try to continue influencing their loved ones. As this only seems possible by draining their energy, those left behind can find themselves chronically debilitated, a condition that can miraculously vanish once the deceased person in question has gone into the light, as related in many cases studies in this book. I strongly encourage people to read this book and apply its insights to their own life journey.

David Lorimer — Programme Director *Scientific and Medical Network*

⁓✳︎⁓

Doctors, ministers and therapists will find much of value in this book. The instructive and sensitively written text highlights the subtle effects of bereavement within the family, gives informative case histories and indicates that spirit attachment is a common condition. Meditation and persistent sensitive talk to the earthbound spirit is a highly effective treatment. This republishing of the little-known *The Bright Light of Death*, by Annabel Chaplin, a close colleague of Phyllis Krystal, is an important event. The new Introduction by Anne Baring, Jungian analyst, soul-focused philosopher and historian, is admirable.

Dr Alan Sanderson — Psychiatrist

Publishers Note

As our consciousness has evolved in the intervening years since Annabel first wrote this book, so too have the influences of dogma and doctrine on our thinking diminished. We have also benefited from research and are hopefully more aware of our own shadow material viewing ourselves and others with compassion rather than judgement and condemnation. Hence the reason for inviting Anne Baring to write a new Introduction.

For the New Edition, 2019

During our efforts to contact the author, we were informed by the original publishers, DeVorss and Co., that the 'rights' had reverted to the author before her death in 2002. Ongoing attempts to contact Annabel's family have so far drawn a blank so we would be pleased to receive any help in this process and will gladly acknowledge the outcome in any future editions.

For details of all our titles and backlist go to:

www.archivepublishing.co.uk

RELEASE

into the

LIGHT

*...a continuation of life and
the soul's journey*

Annabel Chaplin

ARCHIVE
publishing

First published in 1977 as *The Bright Light of Death*
by DeVorss & Company, Publishers,
Marina Del Rey, California.

This New Edition
Published in 2019 in the United Kingdom by
Archive Publishing
Shaftesbury, Dorset, England.

Designed at Archive Publishing by Ian Thorp

Text © 1977 Annabel Chaplin

A CIP Record for this book is available from
The British Cataloguing in Publication data office

ISBN 978-1-906289-49-2 (Paperback)

Cover painting by Frances Crawford

www.archivepublishing.co.uk

Printed and bound by Lightning Source (UK) Ltd

To My Daughters

Acknowledgements
to the First Edition, 1977

There are a few special people to whom I would like to offer a personal note of appreciation for their valuable contribution.

To Dr. Viola P. Neal — without whose encouragement and wise guidance, this book would not have been written.

To Dr. Schafica Karagulla — for her help and support.

To P. — in loving recognition of the time spent together in work and study.

To my husband — for his enthusiasm, patience, and practical suggestions.

To those who are mentioned in this book, many of whom urged the writing and expressed a willingness to share their experiences in order to help others.

To one and all I am indebted. I am deeply grateful.

In all cases the people in this book have been given names other than their own. Superficial identifying characteristics have also been changed to protect client identity.

to the New Edition, 2019

Much thanks to the artist, Frances Crawford for allowing us to use one of her beautiful paintings for the front cover.
www.francescrawfordart.com

Table of Contents

Chapter		Page

A Psalm of Life

Tell me not, in mournful numbers,
Life is but an empty dream!
For the soul is dead that slumbers,
And things are not what they seem.

Life is real! Life is earnest!
And the grave is not its goal;
Dust thou art, to dust returnest,
Was not spoken of the soul.

Not enjoyment, and not sorrow,
Is our destined end or way;
But to act, that each tomorrow
Find us farther than today.

Art is long, and Time is fleeting,
And our hearts, though stout and brave,
Still like muffled drums, are beating
Funeral marches to the grave.

In the world's broad field of battle,
In the bivouac of Life,
Be not like dumb, driven cattle!
Be a hero in the strife!

Trust no Future, howe'er pleasant!
Let the dead Past bury its dead!
Act, — act in the living Present!
Heart within, and God o'erhead!

Lives of great men all remind us
We can make our lives sublime,
And, departing, leave behind us
Footprints on the sands of time; -

Footprints, that perhaps another,
Sailing o'er life's solemn main,
A forlorn and shipwrecked brother,
Seeing, shall take heart again.

Let us, then, be up and doing,
With a heart for any fate;
Still achieving, still pursuing,
Learn to labour and to wait.

Henry Wadsworth Longfellow

Introduction
to the First Edition, 1977

This is an age of broadened horizons of the mind and of the spirit. We are beginning to realize that there are higher dimensions of environment and of experience which condition our everyday living far more than we have known.

Many people are accepting the truth that there is no death as we have understood that term; that in fact we move out of the physical body into higher dimensions of livingness and awareness. The ancient Egyptians often referred to those living in a physical body as "the entombed," their consciousness shrouded and darkened by the enveloping physical form. I know from my own experience that this is so. The clarity of mind when one is gaining release from the physical body at the point of death and moving into these higher dimensions of Reality is a shining joy and a great illumination. To be pulled back is a weariness and a sadness at first, but accepted as a part of the total life experience. I know surely that one cannot complete that journey until it is one's time and destiny to do so.

Those who do not know that the experience called death is merely a moving through a bright door into a greater and happier Reality are often earthbound. Their faces are still turned toward the physical world. They become tied to those living in the physical body, to the detriment of themselves and those they leave behind.

Annabel Chaplin has had many years of experience assisting the earth-bound, and their loved ones left behind, to find release into freedom. Many of her readers will find answers to baffling experiences that have troubled them for years. She speaks with a compassion and sincerity that cannot be questioned. She has a clear direct style of writing and an intuitive ability to anticipate and answer the questions in the minds of her readers. This book is an important contribution to the emerging knowledge which is dissipating an age-old fear of the human race.

Viola Petitt Neal, Ph.D (London)

Foreword
to the First Edition, 1977

I have been led to write this book by a series of events and dreams which I could not ignore. Whenever I inwardly protested that I did not want to write a book, I was invariably shown in dreams, sequentially corroborated by an event in life, that my personal reluctance was of no importance. Whenever I hesitated, someone innocently prodded me into action by a request for the kind of help described in this book.

There were many personal reasons why I held back. I could justify my reasons and support my position, but I could not deny the inner teaching, the inner directions.

Over the years I have observed that many people are in the kind of trouble described in this book. It is to these people that the contents of the book is directed.

Annabel Chaplin

Introduction
to the New Edition, 2019

It could be said that fear of death is the principal neurosis of humanity. In the forty or so years since this book was first published, with the title of *The Bright Light of Death*, much has changed but not enough to address this neurosis and make a real difference to people's lives. There is a pervasive silence about death in our culture and a tendency to censor or disparage anything that is designated as 'non-rational'. So extreme has this neurosis become that the technological dream of some scientists is to prolong the life of the physical body indefinitely, thereby giving them the god-like power to eliminate death from the human experience. They even aspire to create a new species that would be immortal and endowed with superhuman intelligence. The moral implications of these initiatives to defeat death by technological means are alarming and abhorrent and far removed from what *Release into the Light* is about. Millions of people in a secular culture believe that this life is all there is and have no awareness that there is a life beyond death, thereby depriving their lives of trust in their survival and above all, continued relationship with those who have passed on. Consequently, the greatest sorrow they may experience in their lives is the loss of a beloved parent, partner or child, believing they may be lost to them forever. A small child's loss of his mother is the greatest trauma he or she may endure, with life-long consequences.

I am certain that this new edition of Annabel Chaplin's book could be of great help to those who have suffered these tragic losses as well as to those who are nearing the end of their lives. The more we open our minds to the fact of our survival and explore what lies beyond death, the more trust in our continued existence will grow and the more prepared we will be for our own transition and that of those close to us and the more we will understand the meaning and value of our lives on this planet. Annabel Chaplin's own story describes how she came to trust her intuition and her experience as a therapist to develop her ability to contact those who needed help, whether in this world or the one beyond. Her book could be of enormous assistance to others who find themselves in the same position but do not know how to help their loved ones move into the Light.

While reflecting on how to write this Introduction in a way that would do justice to her book, I had the following dream:

I dreamt I was in a hotel in an unspecified place. I went down to the lower ground floor and found a small tree unexpectedly growing there. Hanging from its branches were many enormous fruits which I thought at first were pomegranates, then found that they were more like ripe peaches — pale pink and golden but much larger than their usual size. Some fruits that I tried to pick seemed to be bruised or past their state of ripeness. I found two that were perfect and picked them, holding them carefully in my cupped hands as they were surprisingly heavy. Later, I found myself at a table with a group of women whom I knew. I cut the peaches/pomegranates into sections and gave them to the women to eat.

This dream had strong associations to the ancient goddess cultures where the pomegranate was a symbol of fertility and the regeneration of life and even, in some cultures, immortality. There is an ancient legend in China that there was a Mother who existed before heaven and earth came into being. She took the form of an immense tree that grew in the Garden of Paradise and supported the whole universe. The fruit of this marvellous tree bestowed immortality on whoever tasted it.

Because of these associations with which I had long been familiar through my own researches and writing, I felt this dream was a confirmation that I should trust what I would write in this Introduction.

All of us are climbing an evolutionary ladder leading to greater and greater consciousness and understanding. Cosmologists have given us a revelation about the staggering size and beauty of the visible universe and its hundred billion galaxies but do we know that we are gazing into a universe which has an inner life as well as an outer form: a universe that is alive, conscious, and the ground of our own consciousness? We have been told by science as a matter of irrefutable fact that consciousness originates with the physical brain and the death of the brain is therefore the end of consciousness. This has, for many of us, created a kind of firewall that has closed our minds to the existence of the abundant evidence that has been gathered over the last 150 years about our survival beyond death — evidence that amounts to a different kind of revelation.

For tens of thousands of years Indigenous (shamanic) cultures have known that there is no death and that we are not alone in the universe. They have known that there is a bridge of connection between this world and the unseen reality which permeates and interacts with our own. The greatest spiritual teachers of all cultures have testified to the existence of this reality, have experienced the higher dimensions of it. Some may even have come to this planet from them. Greece had the Eleusinian Mysteries that gave initiates trust in their survival. Long before Greece, Egypt had a very detailed description of the journey of the soul after death. Far from seeing death as extinction, the Egyptians saw death as a journey towards awakening to cosmic life and the invisible dimension of reality that they called the *Dwat*. Ultimately, their soul could move into a fully awakened state as a shining body of light. In this light-body, the soul could access the higher cosmic planes associated with the sun and the stars. The Egyptians described this experience as "Coming forth into the Day".

Like the Egyptians of 4000 years ago, the Tibetans are a shamanic culture and are aware of the fact that death is a transition to another level of reality. Sogyal Rinpoche tells us in *The Tibetan Book of Living and Dying*, that "All the greatest spiritual traditions of the world, including Christianity, have told us clearly that death is not the end. But despite their teachings, modern society is largely a spiritual desert where the majority believe that this life is all that there is. Without any real or authentic faith in an afterlife, most people live lives deprived of any ultimate meaning." [1]

The Hindus, as well as the Tibetans, believe in reincarnation.

Christians may not know that reincarnation was once part of Christian beliefs and teaching until 553 CE when the Emperor Justinian declared it to be anathema and forbade any mention of it. For nearly 1500 years, this belief has not been part of Christian teaching. Yet so many questions, so many injustices can never be answered or resolved in the context of one life. So many loving relationships are left hanging in the air. One brief life bounded by the fear of impending death enormously increases anxiety, the desire for power and control and the fear and pain of loss, especially if we are told that the death of the physical body is the end of consciousness.

This is why Annabel Chaplin's book is of such immense value at the present time. It follows on from those of Elisabeth Kübler-Ross who was one of the greatest pioneers in opening up the subject of life beyond death. Like the stunning impact of Rachel Carson's book *Silent Spring* in 1962, which alerted us to the danger of what we were doing to the Earth, the publication of Kübler-Ross' book *On Death and Dying* in 1969, tore away the veil that had shrouded the subject of death.[2] She was a doctor and a psychiatrist who, almost single-handedly, helped by her strong personality as well as her extensive clinical experience, transformed attitudes towards death and the care of the dying.

Many of her dying patients told her that their near-death (NDE's) and out-of-the-body experiences (OBE's) gave them trust in their survival and their reunion with loved ones. Increasingly fascinated by these accounts, she reviewed the case-histories of over twenty thousand people from all over the world and every cultural and social background, most of whom had had NDE's and death bed visions. Some had returned to life after being declared clinically dead. To her, the death of the physical body was like the shedding of a worn-out casing or cocoon, releasing the 'butterfly' of the soul into life in another dimension. These thousands of testimonies convinced her that there is no such thing as death: "Only the body dies. The self or spirit is eternal." Thanks to the rapid dissemination of her ideas through her books and seminars, many thousands, if not millions of people were encouraged to have a greater trust in their own and their loved ones' survival after death.

Her books were followed in 1975 by Raymond Moody's phenomenal best-seller, *Life After Life*, giving many accounts of people who survived the experience of clinical death.[3] Since then, many hundreds of testimonies of near-death experiences have given us moving evidence of people's encounter with another dimension of reality and their realisation that we survive death. It is precisely the gift of trust in our survival and how to direct our soul and those of others to the Light that Annabel Chaplin gives us, a trust that is sorely needed when we turn to two of the greatest problems in our society: depression and suicide.

Depression, as we know, is now a major problem worldwide, affecting more and more people, including some 80,000 children and adolescents in the United Kingdom (2018). Millions of people suffering from depression are treated with anti-depressants to the extent that this form of treatment has developed into a virtual epidemic. [4] In a secular culture where there is no longer belief in the existence of God or the soul people in a state of despair may be convinced that there is no-one and nothing that could help them. With regard to children, it is becoming increasingly clear that social media is fuelling a mental crisis that can lead them into depression and even drive them to take their own lives or the lives of others, as in the recent school shootings in America.

Most people do not know that in the not so distant past attitudes to suicide were uniformly dismissive and condemnatory. In Christian culture, suicide was considered to be a sin against God, destroying the life that was given by Him. Suicides were even denied a Christian burial. Later, the State, following the lead of the Churches, made suicide a crime. The family of a suicide could have all their assets stripped and given to the government and end up paupers as well as having to face public opprobrium. In recent years attitudes have changed and become more compassionate and forgiving. In 1961 suicide in the United Kingdom was declared to be no longer a crime. In the United States in 30 out of 50 states there are now no laws opposing suicide or attempted suicide. All states have laws stating that assisted suicide is a felony, but prosecutions are rare.

There were 5,821 suicides in the UK in 2017 and of these the majority were men. Among those who ended their lives were 200 children. In the United States, suicide is the second leading cause of death for children, adolescents, and young adults, resulting in about 4,600 lives lost each year. In addition to these deaths more than 34,000 adults commit suicide in the United States each year.

Worldwide, the statistics from the World Health Organisation for 2017 show that close to 800,000 people commit suicide every year. Every one of these carries a story of human tragedy.

Parents who have lost children through suicide experience the unbearable anguish of losing their sons and daughters, often with no warning, sign or symptom of what is about to befall them. Grandparents who may have lovingly helped these children to grow up are equally affected. While the insidious pressures of social media can contribute to the depression and suicide of children, so too can the loss of a parent, violence or sexual abuse in the home, sadistic bullying by other children at school and on mobiles (cell phones) and the pressure of exams and a sense of failure which may come from trying to adapt to an unbalanced and driven narcissistic 'celebrity' culture. Children, with their still fragile sense of self and limited perspective on life, are particularly vulnerable. There is also the modern scourge of drugs and the addiction to them that can lead to mental illness and ultimately to suicide. The absence of any true foundation for values in modern secular culture together with the break-up of the parental relationship and the loss of one parent can leave the child or adolescent with no sense of the intrinsic value of his or her life. They have no compass for orienting themselves to a sense of inner worth which could help them withstand these pressures and keep them in proportion. Apart from the love and care of their parents, there is nothing in the culture that could help them to access the awareness that their lives hold infinite value and meaning. Psychological insight over the last hundred or so years has brought greater understanding of the childhood traumas that may drive a person to depression or to drug or alcohol addiction and, ultimately, suicide but there is still a long way to go before we can call ourselves a truly compassionate society as well as an enlightened and well-balanced one.

There are other categories of people in our stressed and driven society who feel overwhelmed by despair when rejected by their parents or partners or by financial losses, failed businesses, debt incurred through addiction to gambling or because they feel they can no longer cope with the difficulties of their lives. Some may have their health and mental stability affected by illness, alcoholism and drug addiction. Others cannot endure living with the memories of the traumas they have experienced, such as their sexual abuse as children by teachers or priests.

In a society with an ageing population there are people who may spend years as victims of a debilitating illness with no way out, feeling themselves a burden on their children and with no financial resources to assist them, or fearful of being consigned to a care home where the care offered is inadequate. Suicide for some may offer a way out.

There is also a new category of young men and women who, driven by religious belief, choose the path of martyrdom in the act of destroying the lives of others in horrific ways. Indoctrination, particularly of the unstable, idealistic and vulnerable young, can lead them to these terrible acts, mistakenly believing that in destroying their own life and those of others, they are serving God.

Finally, there is a neglected category of people who may be driven beyond endurance to take their life: the veterans of recent wars. Edward Tick in his deeply moving book, *War and the Soul*, has written with great clarity and compassion about the effect of war on young men and women — something we would do well to remember in view of the many young lives still being sacrificed in ongoing conflicts. Veterans can, he says, be haunted for years by reliving in nightmares and flash-backs the original terrifying experiences they underwent.

They may see themselves killing again, or friends and enemies dying again. They may have waking visions of dead friends, enemies, or both. They may also, in retrospect, feel moral anguish that the people they killed did not deserve to die. [5]

They may suffer from insomnia, frightening mood swings and surges of anger in response to something that to others would be innocuous. They may have to endure living their young lives without the limbs that have had to be amputated, without sight if they have been blinded, without the capacity to develop into the full potential of what they might have been. All this gives rise to intolerable anguish and suffering for both veterans and their families which can endure for years.

In a secular culture where there is no longer belief in the existence of God or the soul people may be convinced that there is no-one and nothing that could help them. They may say to themselves: "I can't see the point of continuing any longer in this miserable existence. Life holds nothing for me but pain and suffering, struggle, loneliness and depression. I am going to make an end to it."

Anyone in the situations outlined above may be too traumatised to realise that, however difficult, their life is of infinite value and some may be drawn to terminate it in order to gain release from a depressed state of mind or an unhappy life that seems to offer no hope of change. But the decision to end one's own life should never be taken except as a very last resort, when all possible options for remaining in this world have been considered. The late Stephen Hawking is an example of the immense courage needed to stay in this life despite facing the enormous challenge of a severely debilitating disease for which there was no cure. Because of this courage, the gift of his extra-ordinary discoveries to humanity and the scientific community has been incalculable.

We may wonder what happens to all these souls when they pass through the portal of death, carrying with them the burden of their despair. Our culture as a whole, whatever our religious beliefs or the absence of them, is starved of information about the after-life. As there is no awareness of life beyond death or any preparation for it in our culture, the realisation that one is still 'alive' in a new and unfamiliar world and that there is no way to reverse the action one has taken may come as a devastating shock. Never having encountered the idea that the death of the physical body is not the end of life for the soul, they may experience bewilderment and even terror when they find they are not dead as they thought, but are still conscious in a different world where they can no longer communicate as they did before with people in the world they have left behind. Knowing nothing of the existence of the Light and the need to seek it out, they may have difficulty finding their way into its Presence and instead remain fixated in a state of profound confusion, regret, fear and despair, unable to move on in this new and unfamiliar environment. They may cling to the emotions that may have driven them to suicide. These powerful emotions do not go away when we die but are taken with us, so to speak, and need to be faced after our death when we

experience a life review which shows us the light and dark aspects
of how we have lived our lives. Who will help these bewildered
souls if they cannot help themselves?

The accounts that have come through over the last 150 years
and are available for all to read suggest that relatives and friends
may come to help souls whose physical existence has been terminated — either by suicide or sudden death — to find their way
to the Light. There are also souls who act as shamanic guides
or psychopomps — whose specific training or vocation both in
this world and the one beyond is to help those who are moving
from one dimension to another to orient themselves in this
new environment. Some who have deliberately ended their life
may need to adjust to the fact that they cannot go back to the
life they knew however much they regret what they did. Others
will need time to recover from the shock of being suddenly
expelled from a familiar world through an accident, terminal
illness, a heart-attack, stroke or any situation which has exposed
them to death in the theatre of war — from bombs, missiles
or lethal chemicals as in the recent wars in the Middle East.
Included in these sudden deaths are the thousands of refugees
who have drowned trying to escape from Libya or Turkey as well
as those murdered in the horrific mass-shootings in American
schools. Those indoctrinated young men and women who have
deprived innocent people of their lives in a violent act of self-
destruction may find things are not how they have been described
by those who drove them to this act. They may remain in a state
of rage, disillusioned bitterness and shame for some time.

Those who have committed suicide as well as those who have
died unexpectedly in their sleep, or suddenly without warning in

an accident or in a war situation, may not realise they have left their physical body and may cling to the life they had in this world and to the people closest to them. They may be held in a state of grief, bewilderment, regret, fear or anger until they are helped to move towards the Light by others on the other side who have become aware of their plight or by relatives and friends in this world who can help to send them to the Light, as this case-history illustrates:

A young woman I will call Jan came to see me feeling unwell and 'not herself'. She had been told she was clinically depressed; anti-depressant medication had helped but she was still 'not herself'. I was struck by her use of the phrase.

Going into her history, I learned that a few months before the symptoms began, Jan's friend had killed herself in Jan's home, having been staying there while my patient was away on holiday. By the time Jan got back, everything had been tidied up and the funeral had already taken place.

Remembering how Jan had twice said she was 'not herself', I asked her if she had the feeling of someone else when she came back home. Jan replied that she hadn't wanted to mention it in case I thought she was mad, but every time she went into the house she had the physical sensation that her friend was right there in the room with her.

Taking this at face value, I asked if Jan would like me to invite the spirit of her deceased friend to the consultation to see if we could get some further clues. She was willing, so I asked her to close her eyes, tune in to her friend and try letting her friend speak through her.

Jan's friend 'came through' and went on to express deep regret at having taken her life. Suicide had solved nothing. She remained lonely, unhappy, and seeking comfort. I explained that staying on was having a bad effect on my patient, and was doing nothing for herself either.

   She apologised. 'If only I had known', she said, 'what I know now. I was facing the biggest challenge of my life and I went and messed it up. I feel even worse than I did before'. I said I was sure other opportunities would be given her. She was very relieved to hear this and we talked more about her hopes for another chance at life. When she said she was ready to move on, I asked her to look for the Light. She exclaimed with a smile 'Yes, I can see it' and left at once. The moment she went, my patient felt the burden of oppression lift from her and it did not return. [6]

   In recent years there have been changes in our understanding — hugely expanded through YouTube as well as books like this — helping people to realise that death is not the end but to see it as the shedding of the physical body prior to entering a different kind of existence. In near-death experiences (NDE'S), many have left their physical bodies and have returned to them inspired and enlightened by what they have seen and experienced. Some have been miraculously healed of terminal cancer and other illnesses.[7] They have glimpsed the joy and the beauty of that other dimension of life. They have met with former partners, parents or friends. They may have seen a glorious figure of Light and have realised that death is not an end but a portal to a new phase of life. [8]

   What is slowly emerging is the realisation that life is an alchemical process of transformation which, however challenging the situations we face, offers an opportunity to discover our creative potential and the reason why we may have chosen to return to this planet not once but many times. Breakdown and severe depression can sometimes lead to breakthrough to a new level of understanding: the discovery of a new way of living life. In spite of all its suffering, challenge and struggle, life in a physical body remains the greatest opportunity for spiritual and emotional growth and transformation. We are here to learn, to discover, to grow into our full potential, to develop our capacity for love. Sometimes, the very difficulties and challenges we experience are helping us to develop skills and resources we would not have discovered without them. When we are young we cannot possibly know what experiences lie ahead and how these may transform our understanding and lead to the discovery of our creative gifts and responsibilities. To cut short our journey in the physical world in childhood, adolescence or in our twenties and thirties may leave unfulfilled the purpose for which we were born. Because the pain of living seems unbearable, we may leave this world too soon.

If we have the knowledge that our life does not end with the death of the physical body, we can trust and hope that we will be led to whatever situation in the world beyond is best for the growth of our understanding and further spiritual development as well as our creative gifts and interests. We can trust that we will have help and support and that we will find our way — as Annabel Chaplin tells us — into the Presence of the Light. We are immortal souls, an intrinsic part of the divinity of Life. We have a role to play in the service of Life on this planet and beyond it, in other dimensions or spheres of reality. So much suffering, so much depression and so many suicides could be prevented if we were aware of this and could trust in our existence here and our survival there.

How can we imagine life beyond death? We need to imagine the invisible planes of reality filled with concentric belts, spheres or zones of matter far finer than the composition of our world and varying in vibratory frequency. What separates them from each other and makes them invisible to us is the faster or slower vibrational rate of each level, world or sphere. Billions of souls inhabit these spheres or zones, attracted to the level that relates to their spiritual development and their specific culture or focus of interest. Underlying and permeating this plethora of worlds is the Light and Love of the divine ground which emanates from the highest world and permeates and sustains all worlds, all levels of reality.

The cosmic ground of being is an immeasurable ocean of Light and Love. Each one of us, each element of life is the creation, the embodiment, the carrier of that love. Light in the higher worlds does not come from the sun but from this ineffable source of Light. The closer the zones or spheres are to the source, the more radiant they are. The beauty of the higher, inner or finer zones is indescribable. Our world is permeated and sustained by this cosmic Light and Love. We may not be able to see or feel it until with meditative practice we begin to become aware of it.

Each of us has several bodies corresponding to different levels or planes of reality:

1. We have a physical body for this material world.

2. We have a soul body within or, some say, surrounding

the physical body, sometimes called an etheric or astral body, composed of much finer particles than the physical body but resembling it exactly. At the point of death this soul body emerges from the physical body and is connected to it by a silver cord. Death ensues when the silver cord is severed from the physical body. This soul body can move freely; it can create form through thought and imagination alone. It communicates telepathically. When we discard the physical body our soul body comes into its own and we discover to our surprise that we are not 'dead' but very much alive in a 'body' which has the same features as our old one but in a more youthful and healthy state. In this soul body we can see and hear as before, only more intensely. We have instantaneous access to the thoughts of others as well as to places or people whom we wish to see or communicate with. To some extent we can visit other planes of that subtle reality but we cannot visit the higher realms for very long until our soul vibrations have become attuned to the finer vibrations of that plane of reality.

3. Thirdly, we have a spirit body of finer particles that corresponds to more evolved states of consciousness that are gradually activated as we move closer and closer to the Light of the divine ground. We carry our soul and spirit body within us. The unrecognised divinity at the 'core' our being is what Jesus called "The pearl of great price".

What does the experience of moving from one dimension of reality to another feel like? Here is a description from a man who was considered to have been clinically dead for twenty-three minutes. This was included in a book by Dr Marie-Louise von Franz called *On Dreams and Death* which suggests that when we die we move into a field that vibrates at a faster rate than our own:

"I was moving very quickly toward a bright shining net which vibrated with a remarkable cold energy at the intersecting points of its radiant strands. The net was like a lattice which I did not want to break through. For a brief moment my forward movement seemed to slow down, but then I was in the lattice. As I came in touch with it, the light flickering increased to such an intensity that it consumed and, at the same time, transformed me. I felt no pain.... From then on everything was different.... The whole thing was like a transformer, an energy-transformer, which transported me into a formlessness beyond time and space. *I was not in another place — for spatial dimension had been abolished — but rather in another state of being."* [9]

Another account of our parting with the physical body describes how, "As quietly as the dawn meets morning, the separation comes. Out of the housing of the flesh, the inner body emerges, and it is welcomed by those who have gone before. There are mid-wives on the other side, waiting to assist with our birth into that other dimension. This is the second birth, so like the first, except that all the knowledge, individuality and spirituality gained in our earth life is retained, and we live on in the fullness of our mentality and strength as before. Dissolution neither adds to nor subtracts from the sum total of our knowledge. The inner body in which we have functioned, we shall still function in for all eternity." [10]

Suppose we knew beyond any possibility of doubt that our soul is immortal, that the finality of death is the greatest of our illusions and that we return to this planet countless times in the course of our evolutionary journey. Suppose we knew that death is simply a change of worlds and that when we die the soul — the part of us that does not die — enters another reality. How would the perspective on our lives change if we knew that death leads into a world that is as real and tangible as this one, where we are reunited with family and close friends, and can explore, grow and use our creative gifts with a freedom that many of us do not have here? How would we feel if we knew that our passage through death leads us into a vastly expanded life in dimensions or worlds beyond this one? Only by cleansing the doors of perception, as Blake advised us to do, can we become aware of the presence of these transcendent worlds.

We are living in a time of stupendous scientific discoveries which are enlarging our vision of the universe, shattering the vessel of our old concepts about the nature of reality. This is perhaps the most momentous time in our history: a time of the utmost depravity, greed and barbarism but also a time of tremendous opportunity to move to a higher or more complete level of consciousness, recognising that we are inseparably connected to the world around us and the wider universe and that we have a vital role to play in harmonising our culture with the evolutionary intention of the cosmos. The soul of humanity is going through a great transformation and the focus of this transformation is the awakening of the heart. The heart is our bridge to the cosmos. The heart could help us build a bridge between the long-separated dimensions of our experience — the visible and invisible worlds — and open our minds to the awareness that there is only one life, one reality, one consciousness and we are all held in the embrace of Divine Light and Love.

Anne Baring, MA(Oxon), PhD,
Jungian Analyst,
White Lodge, Alresford,
11th January, 2019

Death

Death is so beautiful
That youth beholding him
Counts all the world well lost
To follow him,
Into the radiance of a dawn
More fair than earth has ever known.
And age looks deep into his eyes
And knows
That all the unfulfillment of this life
Is but a passing sorrow
And that fulfillment waits
Beyond his beckoning hand.
Death is so beautiful
That all men follow
Nor look backward
When he calls.

Viola Petitt Neal

Chapter 1

The Dream of Liberation

The first forty-five years of my life I was sound asleep, mechanically obeying any authority figure, going through the motions of living, a will-of-the-wisp, a leaf driven by the winds, a speck of dust — a nothing! Suddenly, without any warning, I was catapulted into another world — the world of reality — a world where everything had meaning, beauty, joy. I was alive! I was awake!

It all began with a dream. I dreamed that I was in a small train, just large enough to hold me. I went down, down, down into what seemed like the bowels of the earth. It was dark except for lights coming out of the many windows of a large three-storied brick building. From where I sat in my train I could peer into the lit-up rooms. I glimpsed a couple, presumably a man and wife, eating: a woman giving birth to a baby: another waiting for her lover. Outside of the building there was a group of people clinging to one another. They looked miserable, cold, almost lifeless. Yet I knew they were not dead. The whole scene was eerie. I was puzzled. My attention was riveted to the people outside the building and I thought, "Poor things. How can they breathe in that awful, dank, stifling atmosphere?" Abruptly I awoke.

I knew the dream had a message for me. I knew that it was important. It haunted me for days on end. At odd moments the subjective feeling of going down and down kept recurring and hitting me in the solar plexus. Time and again the clarity of the bright lights from the windows and the contrasting heavy grey mist on the outside, returned vividly to my memory. And most of all, the still and lifeless people huddled together, clinging to the building, troubled me. The disturbance that the dream caused within me was as bewildering as the dream itself. Why? I had to find out. I searched for help, for an answer to my dream. Some-one said, "I know a psychologist who works with dreams and is particularly helpful to people like you who have learned to meditate."

I had been meditating regularly following my own intuitions. All this happened twenty-one years ago, when meditation was considered a rather strange pursuit and was not as popularly accepted as it is today. In fact, those of us who meditated were considered rather odd and far out.

Acting upon the suggestion I went to the psychologist and told him about my dream. He had an unusual method which led the dreamer into completing the dream and resolving the hidden message. He sat opposite me and we meditated together. I felt peaceful and relaxed, as I often do in meditation. He spoke quietly. "Tell me again your dream, but this time don't stop. Let the dream continue; keep going." [1]

I did as he requested. I came to the part of the dream where I had seen the people in the stifling air clinging to each other. As I watched, one figure clothed in a long dark robe emerged. I gasped! That figure was myself! I became one with that black-robed figure! I was no longer the observer in the train — I was that person struggling for breath and choking.

Desperately I tried to pull away from the people who were holding me, smothering me. They wouldn't let go. I screamed — horrible hoarse screams! I was in an agony of pain. This was the end of me! The people became like wild animals who were tearing me apart. I was being cut to pieces. The medieval torture rack was stretching my body. I screamed and screamed, and screamed — dear God!!

Suddenly with one last wrenching effort I broke loose. I was free! I was flying away from that awful place. I looked back. Below me I saw a large black whirling ball. A moment ago I was inside that black ball, in a prison of horror, attached to fiendish beings. Now I was floating off into the blue sky, the purified air, the warm bright sun. It was sheer joy — ecstasy — freedom.

All this time the psychologist had remained in meditation. I had to experience the pain of rebirth without interference. He sensed this and did not interrupt. Later I recalled having experienced similar pains when I gave birth to my oldest daughter and the joy and relief when I held her in my arms.

I left the psychologist's office full of gratitude, but by the time I reached home I could barely function. I crawled into bed and stayed there for several days. I was completely drained. Relief? Yes. Joy? Yes. Sad? Yes. Everything and nothing. I read Kahlil Gibran and was comforted.

At the end of three days I revived and became myself again. Myself? Never the same self; the old self was gone. I was different. I knew it. Others saw it and questioned me. I said nothing. The new me was something I had to get accustomed to. I was no longer interested in my former activities — golf, the country club, entertaining, clothes. All this seemed boring and unimportant.

I yearned to know more about the Higher Life of which I had had only a glimpse. I went to lectures on all subjects spiritual and esoteric. I was hungry for knowledge and understanding. I knew beyond a question of doubt that there was more to life than what appeared on the surface. I joined groups. I studied. I asked. I searched. And always I meditated — always the greatest learning, the most profound teaching, came from my meditations, my dreams and mental images. The books and lectures stimulated my mind, but any original thoughts or direction came from the inner self, from the inner teaching. In fact I can never take personal credit for what I am about to relate. Whatever I experienced from that day to this, whatever I have learned, whomever I have been privileged to help, has been the result of the wisdom of this inner teaching.

My Dream of Liberation had taught me the deeper meaning of freedom. It taught that in order for each one of us to function to the fullest capacity, it is necessary to be free — free from guilt, fears, anger, resentments. In my case I had to be free from the people who had chained me to them. Chains of possessive love can be just as binding and destructive as chains of hate. The end result is the same — a stifling of the soul, of the personality, of the body.

Prior to my dream I had had difficulty with ordinary breathing and spoke heavily through my nose. I habitually walked around with my mouth open. I was close to being asthmatic and many a night awoke gasping for breath. After my Dream of Liberation, this outer manifestation disappeared, never to return. But what happened to me, the real person, was of far greater importance than the physical healing. The Dream had freed the soul, the real self. I was free to grow and to learn, free to make my own mistakes without blaming others. I studied Ouspensky and Nicoll and learned to observe myself objectively. Although I didn't like what I observed, I learned compassion for myself and others. I learned the importance of facing up to the negative aspects, working on and releasing them.

As time went on, unexpectedly many people came to me for counseling. Although a subsequent dream revealed that this was going to happen, I was truly surprised when so many came 'knocking on my door'. Recognizing the importance of helping them obtain their freedom as I had, I probed for their particular chains and tried to help them sever their ties. And invariably I asked about their dreams and often found within them their own "Dream of Liberation" — their way to freedom.[2]

Practically it is not an easy matter to 'look within.' Techniques do exist, however, and until recently religion seemed to have a monopoly on them. Spiritual meditation has always been the gateway to a special kind of self-knowledge, and, certainly, a rich reward awaits the contemplative soul.

Joshua Loth Liebman — *Peace of Mind*

Chapter 2

The Moon People

I heard of a therapist who worked with his clients using mental imagery and meditation techniques.[1] I decided to see him. For many personal reasons, I worked with him for only a few short months. He was intrigued by the ease with which I entered the deeper dimensions of the mind, and we had many interesting sessions. He remarked one day after an unusual episode that my mental images showed an inclination and ability to explore the unknown and to reach higher dimensions of the mind. He thought I was destined to do something original. His comment meant nothing to me then and only now, as I am about to relate some extraordinary experiences in working with the dead, do his words come back to me.

It is important to state here and now that all mental images that I have ever experienced were in full waking consciousness. Never have I been in the trance state. I always knew who I was and where I was. The mental images seem to come from a source beyond my everyday knowledge, sometimes symbolical, sometimes very factual. For me it seems to come in sequential pictures and symbols as though there were a movie projector inside my mind operating from a higher source. One picture follows another and

I never know what is coming next. Rarely have I time to question. I am too engrossed in watching the rapidly moving pictures.

With a little guidance many people can experience this method of learning. Some have a more natural aptitude for it than others, but it can be taught. Like meditation, one has to relax the physical body and the outer mind before slipping into that other dimension which appears to be what Jung calls a waking dream, or active imagination.[2]

Although the messages from the inner level of imagery were profound and sometimes puzzling, when they were understood the meaning became clear and the solution fairly simple. Over and over again the learning from the inner level came in these words, "Keep it simple." Usually the remedy was, and often is, quite truly simple.

On one particular day I entered this higher dimension of mind which produced in imagery personal recollections of my early childhood and girlhood. Just as I was about to come to the end of the session, I entered a deeper dimension of mind which evoked a more cosmic picture. I was suspended between the sun and the moon, standing on a floating disk on which I felt secure. I gravitated toward the moon, but the therapist kept urging me to go to the sun. However, the moon environment magnetised my disk and I kept going down, down, down. As I came closer to the moon I could see countless numbers of little people there. They saw me approaching and came running from their hiding places, gesturing with their hands, pleading and begging, "Take me, take me, take me!" The therapist interrupted, again instructing me to go back to the sun.

I yearned to help these distressed beings on the moon, but

I didn't know what to do for them. Who were these people? What were they doing on the moon? What did it all mean? Their pleas haunted me. The moon, as I interpreted it, was a symbol for the abode of the so-called dead who had lost their way. The inhabitants, living in this condition, seemed to be pleading for help. I believed that I had floated down to their dimension for a specific reason But I needed more experience and knowledge before I could understand the full meaning of their plight and my role. A little later, when I began working on the releasing of the dead who are earth-bound, I learned that there was something that I could do to help the "moon people" step out of that desolate dimension and onto their own disk, to make their own journey to the sun, to the Source.

The therapist was right and what I gained from the personal experience of a trip in symbolic imagery to the sun was valuable. Later, as I meditated on the plight of the "moon people." I began to perceive that the job of rescuing the dead could be dangerous and destructive to me as a person. I learned from my meditation that I must never take anyone on my own disk, that each one has to have his or her own disk, path, or way. And, most of all, I learned never to interfere with anyone's free will!

It was often emphasized that neither I, nor anyone else, could arbitrarily decide what is best for another individual. Each one has the God-given right to make his or her own decision, whatever that may be. Any interference, no matter how well-intended, is fraught with danger. So I learned to wait patiently for the request from persons directly involved before making any attempt to help.

"As above, so below."[3] What is true for the dead is also true for the living. We must allow the other person the liberty of choosing her own path or his freedom of expression. Too many of us in the name of love, over-protect our children. Too many of us in the name of love inflict our desires and ambitions upon our children. In the name of love we are guilty of interfering with their growth process, and in the adult world the male can be over protective of his mate, or the female can be the dominating partner. The 'I know what is best for you' attitude can stifle and choke the loved one. And death does not rectify the situation.

The strong, even after death, often want to govern the weak and imprison the object of their love. The weak do not have the power to step out of their bondage, even after the death of the dominant personality. Their will has been too often surrendered to the stronger person.

The "moon people" seemed to fall into the category of the weak characters. In life and in death they had followed the path of least resistance and had leaned on someone else. Now they wanted to be air-lifted out of their plight. Eventually some were ready and could be assisted to go to a better environmnent. I believe who ever asks for help should be helped. Each should ask.

I decided to dedicate myself to this job, and I know there are others on this side of life, and on the other side of life, who have also chosen this way of service. It took years of training in many ways to bring me to the point of implementing this decision. Eventually I found it was simpler than I had thought.

How hast thou helped the one that
is without power? How savest thou
that arm that hath no strength?

The Bible – Job 26:2

Chapter 3

The Bright Light

As I recall the train of events which led me into this new and strange world, I am amazed how each experience seemed to be systematically arranged from a source beyond me. Step by step a new teaching was constantly being revealed to me on a subject about which I had no previous training or experience. I was continually being exposed to the kind of knowledge necessary for work in the unknown world. The fine hand of destiny, the guiding light of fate were always pushing me toward the goal. I seemed to meet the right people at the right time and experience the exact event needed for the learning process.

At about this time I met a brilliant woman who was using the same method of mental imagery. Finding we had much in common, both of us searching for answers to the complexities of life, both of us accustomed to meditative practices, we decided to work together.

On one particular day we began as usual. It is as vivid in my mind now as it was then, many years ago. My friend, as was her custom, had pen and pad in hand ready to record my inner pictures. We rarely chose the topic for the session but always let the teaching forces decide what was right and best for us to experience at that time. We are convinced that there are teaching forces in the universe and learned to probe that source of knowledge for our basic understanding of the principles of life. We learned to rely on that source of knowledge when we were puzzled by the seeming riddle of life. We learned to seek that source of knowledge to help us solve the unsolvable. We constantly tapped its resources and it never failed to give us the renewed strength needed for the goals we were attempting to reach. This inner source of knowledge stressed service — service to humanity.

On the day I refer to above we settled down for the next step in learning. Serene and relaxed in mind and body, I did not expect what was about to occur.

In imagery I found myself in a most desolate place with no signs of life anywhere. Fallen branches of dead trees were strewn about the parched and arid earth; broken slabs of stone, evidently grave markers, lay scattered over the barren ground. The air was heavy and a gray mist clouded the entire area. I knew that I was in a deserted place, a neglected graveyard, and I solemnly announced, "Today we are going to learn something that has to do with death".

As the inner pictures moved on I left that dreary, desolate place and suddenly came to an entirely different region. I was catapulted from the depressing, barren graveyard into an environment totally the opposite, startlingly beautiful, an area of meticulous design, an architectural work of art, bright with clear light. It was awesome.

I stood in front of a very long, broad flight of stairs. Nowhere in all my travels had I ever seen stairs like these, in breadth and in height they seemed to go on and on. I was standing on the lowest step and in the very center. Directly above me, very high up, sat a glorious figure of such luminosity that it almost blinded me!

Suddenly I was down on my hands and knees in reverent obeisance. I don't know how long I remained in this position, but when I stood up my attention was turned away from the center of light above me to the right side of the stairs. There I saw a long line of black-hooded beings with bowed heads. There were many of them, each on one of the steps holding on to what seemed like a rope. Somehow I knew they had come from the desolate graveyard.

As I watched, one figure, a woman, emerged from behind the ropes. I knew her! It was a friend, Anita, who had died of a heart attack a few months before. She was about fifty years old, a widow, the kind of a woman who had really enjoyed life. She was pretty, vital, witty and fun loving. As I watched her she began to twist herself around the figure of a man. Her gyrations were like a snake, twisting and turning around the body of the helpless man. Her hands were clutching and clawing and grasping in her desire to possess him. Blood flowed from his entire body, which was becoming disfigured and distorted.

It was an ugly sight. I watched horrified! Suddenly I recognized the man — he was alive! I knew him and his wife well. I became concerned and quite upset, for the dead woman's intentions were obvious. While she was alive she had pursued him relentlessly, and now, though dead, her desire for him was as ardent as it had always been.

When she was alive, unresponsive to her persistent advances, he fought her off and could handle the situation. But now that she was invisible and his defenses relaxed, he was in the process of being destroyed by her insatiable desires. He was completely unaware of the danger that was engulfing him. It was obvious what was happening and the awful consequences if Anita were allowed to go on. Instantly and without premeditation I went over to Anita and began talking to her.

For the first time she saw me and seemed not at all surprised to find me there. Like countless others who have died, she did not even seem to know that she had passed on! This is a condition common to those who die suddenly. Gently I told her the circumstances of her sudden death and urged her to release the man as it was impossible for him ever to respond to her passionate desires. I explained to her that he would be strangulated by her hold on him. Since they were on different sides of life, nothing could be accomplished except that he would lose his life force, probably become ill, and she would exist in an endless agony of frustration and unrequited love. As I was communicating with her, her body uncoiled and her hands relaxed their stranglehold on the man. I had her complete attention.

I took one of her hands in mine and walked slowly with her to the center of the steps from where I had originally viewed the entire scene. I never stopped talking. I told her that what was in store for her was far better than clinging to another's soul and body. I kept repeating something I sensed but didn't really know — that the place to which she was being led was beautiful beyond description, a happy place, the right place for her.

The nearer we came to the center where I had initially viewed the Great Being of Light high above, the more willing, almost eager, she became. I was deeply engrossed in talking to her, looking into her eyes, when suddenly a tremendous change came over her. Some thing she experienced was lighting her up. I couldn't see what she was seeing, but her face became bright and luminous, a reflection of that Great Being of Light! I no longer had to cajole her. Some thing she saw must have convinced her even more than my words, for now she was eagerly pressing forward, moving toward the Bright Light. We came to the center divider. I kissed her and said good bye. At that very moment she crossed over the center line, her soul free — free to walk into the Bright Light of Death. She looked radiantly happy.

It was a strange, awesome experience. I was impressed by how the inner teaching had used someone I knew in order to demonstrate the lesson on a subject which otherwise might have been abstruse. The projected lesson stressed the awful hold the dead can have on an unsuspecting living person, and, equally as important, the danger for anyone crossing over to the other side still tied to a desire for the living. Up until this time I had understood the importance of release from various kinds of ties, but this was different. For the first time I was transported into that other dimension of life, called death, in order to realise and know that strong ties continue even after the life force has left the physical body, and that intense desires survive death.

Being of a very practical nature, I wondered how I was to know that in releasing people like Anita a powerful tie was actually severed. Obviously I couldn't check further with Anita, safe in the world beyond, nor could I inform the victim of his near escape from a dangerous attack by the dead. But I could check on the health of the besieged man to find out if he had been as physically and emotionally affected as the inner pictures had indicated.

And so, I contacted his wife and learned that he hadn't been well for the past few months, that he was constantly complaining of pains in his stomach and was unusually irritable and depressed. I questioned the timing of his distress and found that it coincided with the period directly after Anita's death. The wife never suspected my interest in her husband's health. I tried to convey the concern of a friend, but I was really seeking confirmation. Although the inner pictures never failed to teach an important lesson, because of the unusual nature of this experience, I had to be doubly certain.

I continued probing for further evidence and learned that directly after Anita released her hold on the man, his health was restored and he regained his normal vitality. The time period of his distress and subsequent recovery checked out precisely with my experience. When Anita crossed over to her side of life, the victimized man was liberated. In view of such beneficial results I was convinced of the validity and importance of the lesson. It was an unforgettable experience for me and the basis for future work in this dimension.

But if the presentation of this new knowledge had ended with Anita's experience, I would not have become so heavily involved with the problems of the dead and their influence on the living. As though the inner teacher knew that I would be dubious in accepting the lesson without more verifiable evidence, the very next day another unusual situation involving the dead occurred. I was given no time to ponder, to doubt, to weigh the evidence, to forget. I was stunned into acceptance.

It is one of the most beautiful
compensations of this life that
no one can sincerely try to
help another without helping
themselves.

Ralph Waldo Emerson

Chapter 4

The Demand

For a number of years I had been conducting classes in meditation and self-observation. It was my custom to see each one of the group privately once or twice a month, more often if necessary. On the day following my experience with Anita, a recent member of the meditation group, Ella, was due for a personal interview. She was seeking help physically and emotionally. Subject to long periods of depression, Ella had colitis and was extremely nervous. Insomnia was one of her major problems and most of the time even sleeping pills did not help. When I opened the door to receive her, she appeared greatly distressed and fell sobbing into my arms. "Thank God, I had this appointment to see you today. I am in trouble."

I talked quietly to her and she calmed down. And then she threw the bombshell at me! "I had a terrible dream last night. I dreamed that my mother came into bed with me and hugged me so hard, so tightly that she hurt me It was so real!".

I looked at her. "Your mother is dead isn't she Ella?"

"Oh, yes," she replied, "She died seventeen years ago. She was a wonderful woman, and we had a very good relationship. The later years of her life she lived in our home. My husband loved her too;

he was so good to her. After mother died," she continued, "I often felt her presence, particularly when I was in bed or in the kitchen where we had spent many happy hours together preparing the meals. She was never a problem, always a joy."

"But," I asked, "What happened in your dream to distress you so much, dear?"

Ella went on with the dream, "It was terrible! It was so real. At first I enjoyed having her hold me in her arms. I felt like a little girl again. But then, she began to get rough, really rough. She squeezed me so hard that my bones cracked. It was so painful that I cried out to her, 'Stop it, mother, you are hurting me.' And with that she slapped me with such a force that I fell out of bed. As I landed on the floor she shouted, 'Do something about it!' What does the dream mean?" Ella pleaded. "What does she want me to do? What can I do?"

Now it was my turn to be shaken! "Do something about it"? A woman dead for seventeen years demanding help, help from the living, help from us! She couldn't free herself, she evidently didn't know anything else to do but to appeal to her own daughter.

Just twenty-four hours ago I had watched as Anita tried to get a stranglehold on a living person. Just twenty-four hours ago I had seen clearly the power of the dead as they exercised their will to possess or influence someone else. Just twenty-four hours ago I had witnessed the miracle of the Light. I knew that I had to do something. I knew that Ella's coming to me for help at that moment in time was not mere coincidence. Had it been planned? I was dumbfounded.

Inwardly I protested. It was too soon. How did Ella's mother know that I had just learned something that could release her —

or did she know? Did she know that night of the dream that Ella was coming the next day to see me? What kind of grapevine of communication was this? Ella had made a routine appointment a week before the Anita experience. What an operation of events! How weird! Now I *was* shaken. Tremors of fear and awe vibrated through my body. I was such a novice. And yet it seemed that I was supposed to help — "to do something about it." I had to meet the challenge. The knowledge that had been given me was not to be wasted, and so I calmed down. I knew what had to be done. Anita had taught me. Now Ella's mother demanded.

I had much to explain to Ella about dreams and particularly about death. I told her that in her sleep her conscious mind is quieted, and the unconscious mind prevails. In those moments much of the contents of the unconscious come to the surface. In dreams we often receive, in pictures and symbols, important information about ourselves — information and knowledge that we may consciously suppress. It is difficult to understand our own dreams when they come to the surface and even the great Carl Jung admitted that he had difficulty interpreting his own dreams. Often a year or years might elapse before he could understand his dreams.

It is no wonder that we, lacking his enormous talent and training, have great difficulty understanding our dreams. The symbology is precise, but it takes a great deal of knowledge to translate the symbols. The dream pictures are significantly trying to convey to us the truth about ourselves, our predicaments, our hopes and our fears. But when we dream about a dead person, the experience is usually different. First of all, the dead appear quite clearly. There is no vagueness. Many times people say, in speaking of a dream about a dead mother or a dead father, "it was so real". This is a common experience and usually a very comforting one. I remember seeing my own mother in a dream about six months after she died. She looked radiantly happy and young. "It was so real!"

Ella's dream was extra-ordinary for many reasons. She had received bodily bruises. She was slapped and thrown out of bed. She was terrorized! What had formerly been a pleasing happy event became a frightening bewildering experience. The once comforting arms had become bands of steel hurting and bruising her. And then the demand, clear and loud, — "Do something about it!" In otherwords, "Help me. I want to be free. I want to go on. Help me!"

It was a definite command, an awesome challenge which, but for the experience with Anita, would have been as bewildering to me as it was to Ella. But I did understand and knew that I had to apply the knowledge that just twenty-four hours ago I had acquired. Was this a test of my resolve to help the dead and free the living?

I told Ella that I understood the dream and believed that there was something that we could do together to give the help demanded. She didn't seem at all surprised. She trusted me more than I did myself. Her ready acceptance and belief in my ability to help her were incredible, and my own inner feeling that I was in touch with a greater knowledge gave me confidence.

Silently I appealed to the inner level of knowledge for some guidance. We began with a prayer. Ella loved the Twenty-third Psalm, so we said it together. She relaxed and throughout the entire time remained in the calm meditative state, alert and aware, willing and co-operating in the effort to free her mother.

I talked to her mother as though she were actually with us. Maybe she was — I couldn't tell. I am not clairvoyant, but I felt her presence. By this time I too was in that dimension of mind that is calm and free from any self-consciousness. The words that flowed from my heart were expressed in a slow, deliberate, rhythmic cadence. Simply and authoritatively my inner Self spoke to Ella's mother directly. "Your demand for freedom is understood.... You have been frustrated for all these long years.... You are weary.... You long for your own way of life.... You are unhappy about Ella's health.... You sense that your presence is detrimental.... You are right.... Ella and I welcome this opportunity to help release you from bondage".

There was a stillness in the room. A light. A presence. We prayed. The instructions continued, "Go, go to the Bright Light. It is there for you. Follow it. It will guide you. Joy and freedom await you". It was over. With tears running down our cheeks Ella and I sat together in a glorious silence. It was a holy moment.

After Ella left me I sat in a dazed silence for some time. The experience was earth-shaking. I reviewed again the sequence of the events of the past two days; the episode with Anita followed by Ella's visit stirred me to the depths of my being and forced me to search deeply for the significance of the lesson. Was this another isolated experience, or was I going to be called upon again? What was expected of me? Had I grasped the full meaning of those sequential events? How could I go on without some tangible evidence? The mystic in me accepted everything that had occurred, the pragmatist still asked for proof. And I knew that in order to continue in this field of endeavor I had to see results. I knew that I could not go on without proof, tangible proof.

Again I didn't have to wait long before the evidence was established. The results, amazingly clear and convincing, came dramatically soon. For three days after the session, Ella suffered the pangs of sorrow at losing a loved one, a kind of mourning period. But after the three days Ella called and excitedly exclaimed, "I feel marvelous! I don't remember when I have felt so light and happy — as though a heavy weight has been lifted from me. Deep in my heart I feel that all is well with mother too". I told Ella that I was reasonably certain that she would continue to feel physically and emotionally much better and that it would last.

"That would be a miracle," Ella replied. "I hope you are right." She sounded happy but somewhat dubious.

Having been ill, nervous and depressed for so many years, it was difficult for Ella to believe that a dream, a meditation and a prayer could cure her of her many ailments. As time went on, however, and Ella's improvement continued, she accepted the "miracle" as a fact.

The burden had been lifted and Ella completely recovered from her stomach ailments, sleeplessness, and deep depression. To this day, fifteen years later, she is an extremely healthy vital woman. The release was final. For what better evidence could there be that something had happened, when an emotionally and physically ill person was restored to radiant health! Finally, a few months later, Ella dreamed again. This time her mother was dancing in the blue sky — barefoot.

After seventeen long years of bondage, Ella's mother had passed on to her own place in the world beyond — the right place for her, where she belonged and 'lived' not as an interloper but as a free and happy being. The priceless gift of release from an undesirable existence had been finally given to her. Fortunately she had been able to convey her unhappy condition to her beloved daughter, who in turn responded and helped her. She was free, and Ella was free. And I learned a valuable lesson. For not only had I been alerted to the problems created by the dead who do not pass on, but I was being shown a way by which they could be helped.

It had been clearly demonstrated to me how the living were drained of vitality when linked to the dead, and how the dead who are earth-bound, need help from the living. At this point in time I did not know where this newly acquired knowledge would take me. But as the years pass by and the need for this kind of service becomes more and more evident, I am grateful that I have learned what to do and can help.

Your children are not your children,
They are the sons and daughters of
    Life's longing for itself.
They come through, but not from you,
And though they are with you
Yet they belong not to you...

* * * * *

But let there be spaces in your togetherness
And let the winds of the heavens dance between you.
Love one another, but make not a bond of love:
Let it rather be a moving sea between the shores
    of your souls.

              Kahlil Gibran — *The Prophet*

Chapter 5

Release and Freedom

Meantime I was very busily pursuing my other activities. There were always the classes in meditation and self-observation and new people continued to "knock on the door". I must admit that I preferred working with the living. I like people, alive people, and enjoy working with them. Most of those who came had been strangers, but as time went on we became good friends. I loved them. We learned from each other. I stressed the importance of release — all kinds of release — release from fear, anger, hate, envy, guilt, pride, and most of all release from children and release from parents. I taught what I had learned from the other side of life — the deeper meaning of freedom.

My experience with the dead made me realize the necessity of understanding our relationships while still in the physical body. Are we still attached to our mothers? Has the umbilical cord really been cut? Are we still nurturing the rejected child within us, the abused child, the overly protected child? Are we still tied to that inner child of the past? Are we filled with resentments of our parents? Then we must be made aware of this condition and cut-the-ties that bind us.[1]

We must do this now while we are alive so that we can go

forward in life and in death as free beings. For if we do not face these problems now, then we miss the opportunity that life offers us to rectify a destructive situation which continues long after the physical life is over. A man who has been rejected by his mother will most likely look for the mother in every female relationship, and miss the chance of a fulfilled man-woman love. The man smothered by too much mother love runs the risk of abnormality; hate has a similar effect.

All ties should be cut now and must be cut with love and forgiveness. For as long as we are tied to our negative emotions we can't graduate to the next experience. We remain behind, as it were, in the first grade. As long as we are tied to other people, we are hindered and crippled in our efforts to go forward. Many people experience this in their dreams — the crippling experience of crawling through life, dragging the feet chained to desires, love, things. Ties that continue long after the physical life is over.

The most insidious ties are those of possessive love — mainly because love seems so desirable, so beautiful, and so good. But strangely the ties forged by possessive love have as destructive a result as ties of hate — the only difference is that one sounds better and looks better than the other.

I was constantly called upon to help cut the ties between parent and child, husband and wife, and others.[2] I recall particularly one woman who had been completely alienated from her only child, a daughter, by her overly solicitous and domineering 'love'. She smothered the child. The daughter, a woman in her late twenties, resented this attachment and avoided all contacts with the mother, even to the point of discouraging all phone conversations. A friend brought the mother to me and in a few sessions, a disastrous relationship was rectified.

After explaining to her the work of release, which she understood, we visualized in meditation the restricting tie between her and her daughter. In her inner pictures the mother could see that she had tied a noose around her daughter's neck, and with each act of overly solicitous love, she had tightened the rope, causing great pain. In imagery, she cut the noose with a sharp knife, destroyed it, and healed the wounds. The inner operation proved to be successful in restoring a healthy relationship between mother and daughter. Today they are close and devoted friends — the love between them genuine and precious. Both are free agents. This procedure has been used in countless numbers of cases where powerful attachments of a binding kind caused one or the other to be estranged or physically or emotionally weakened.

It is far better to recognize the need for release during the life span than to expect that death will remedy all faults, redress all wrongs, solve all problems. Not so. Death releases the physical body only! All else remains the same, and there is no escape from the thoughts, feelings and desires that dominate the soul and the personality during the life span.

At death the opportunity for growth and development in the physical dimension is terminated, and the learning from the life script is ended. Another kind of learning takes place on the other side of life, but even there we can only go as far as we have allowed our consciousness to develop. Thoughts, feelings, and desires, which we have cultivated on this side of life, are carried over to the other side of life — they rule the choices, determine the path in the life beyond.

Over and over again as I worked for the dead this axiom

proved correct. They, the dead, were just where their predominant thoughts and desires had led them. If during the life span they had no training, no teaching about death, then the event called death was bewildering and frightening. The truly religious ones had an easier time, for they expected to see Jesus, or Buddha, or some great master, or their own parents. That expectation and strong desire led them and guided them, and so they were taken care of.

But if the desire is for the material life, for wealth, for power, then they are stuck on the other side with all their power and wealth and nowhere to spend or express it. Imagine having millions of dollars and no need for money, no need for food, or clothing, or possessions of any kind. Imagine the frustration!

On the other side of life the truly creative people continue their vocations — continue to paint, to write, or compose for the sheer joy of expressing themselves. No longer consumed by the drive for success or material gain, they continue to express themselves as they did during their physical lives. Having no egos to satisfy, their souls join with souls of similar talents without the competitive drive. Just as a bird sings for the joy of singing — a way of expressing his kind — so does the creative spirit express itself in the confluence of like souls.

The same is true of those whose lives have been devoted to other pursuits. Each and all are in the place where their predominant desires have led them. Is it any wonder that those of us who are aware of the life-death cycle are eager to present the point of view that there is a life after death — a life beyond that is determined by what we do in the here and now?

For those of evil acts the other dimension of life will be a nightmare of evil thought forms. Evil attracts evil as good attracts good. In other words, here on earth we already determine by our life's activities the nature of the life in the other dimension. For what we are, our very being, creates the life here and on the other side. We should not fear anything but the results of our own creation. "As a man thinketh in his heart, so is he".

If when we die we automatically go to the land of our desires (called Kamaloka by the Theosophists), then we have to be very selective in life about our desires and attachments. We must be extremely careful. We must learn to enjoy what joys life has to offer without too much attachment. We must detach ourselves from hates and resentments. We must admit our faults, our negative thoughts and feelings, and correct them. If we admit our negativity and refuse to change, then we are tied to these traits for a very long time. If we blame our parents, or our teachers, then we have lost another round in the fight for freedom. It is only when we take full responsibility for our faults with courage and strength that we can begin the process of transformation. Awareness brings growth in consciousness, and that is fulfilling the purpose for which we were born.

I urge my fellow students to confront each negative trait and take that first step toward freedom and growth. We work hard, and the more aware we become, the more we change and develop. I have begun to look upon it as a game, and whenever I find another negative trait in myself I have learned to greet it as a foe who could become my friend. That which horrified me when I began this probing, I later treated as an adventure in learning and in living. Now I am no longer upset when I get the message. I am grateful. And I hope and pray that I won't get careless and miss the point.

We all work together for this goal — the goal of release and freedom. Release and freedom for us the living! Release and freedom for the dead!

The person who, casting off all desires, lives free from attachment; who is free from egoism and from the feeling that this or that is mine, obtains tranquillity.

— *Bhagavad Gita 2.71*

Chapter 6

The Victims

I was never allowed to forget the dead. Even though I preferred to work for and with the living I never forgot my commitment to help the dead. Whenever it was asked of me, I accepted the challenge. The one stipulation was that the request had to come directly from the person involved, for I had been taught never to interfere with the free will of anyone, dead or alive. How many times have I met people, sensed their problem, longed to help them, but could not break the law. I had to wait for their request, for their 'knock on the door.'

Whenever I see Jennifer I think how she nearly missed being rescued. Jennifer is the wife of a highly successful and prominent businessman. She is very beautiful with lovely brown eyes, auburn hair, a golden complexion — as beautiful inside, as the saying goes, as she is outside. I first met her nine years ago. Jennifer's older sister Emily introduced us. Emily was a member of the weekly meditation group, a very dear and loving woman. At the time I first met Jennifer she was about thirty years old, the mother of two, a boy of eight years and a girl of five. She lived in a luxurious home with a swimming pool and a tennis court, which Jennifer rarely used.

By all standards she had everything — beauty, intelligence, wealth, and a devoted husband. On the surface Emily's anxiety seemed unwarranted, but I knew that she would not have insisted, without justification, that I visit Jennifer. Emily felt that as close as she thought she was to her sister, on the deeper level she did not really know her. Jennifer kept her thoughts to herself; she was unusually reserved even with those she loved most. Emily described her as a "private person" and warned me that Jennifer would be politely uncommunicative.

Thus forewarned, I met her and had a sociable chat about art, an interest we shared in common, about politics, and other worldly matters. It was a delightful meeting of the minds. I was enjoying myself thoroughly and hastily concluded that Emily was being overly solicitous when a phone call interrupted our conversation and Jennifer left the room.

In her absence I reviewed the hour and realized that I had conversed with Jennifer the outer person, and like all others around her had no idea what was underneath that lovely exterior. Perhaps, I thought, I should probe a little deeper, if for no other reason than to bring back to Emily a thorough report. I decided that in the brief time remaining I would question more deeply. I sent up a little prayer to the inner teacher for help.

I had learned from Emily much about Jennifer's childhood and background and that it had been a happy one. The mother and father adored the two girls and their brother; they were a closely-knit family. Jennifer was the model daughter and the favorite. She 'wanted to please,' enjoyed it, preferred it, and never felt any need to express independence. This in itself is rare. Today we are being bombarded by the demands of the young for independence.

Devoted parents as well as neglectful ones are being harassed by the same rebellious demand regardless of circumstances or need. Here was someone demonstrating a love for obedience and enjoying dependence. If that was Jennifer's nature, then no one could quarrel with it — she liked being the model child and found it effortless. I could not interfere with her choice, her desire, and her destiny.

When Jennifer returned I brought up the subject of my visit, and we talked about Emily's concern for her. Jennifer smiled, "Emily thinks I should lead a more active life, but I am not a gadabout or a doer. I love reading and being by myself".

I knew that it was more serious than the words conveyed. Emily had given me a picture of a young woman reading, sleeping, relaxing a good portion of the day, and yet rarely feeling energetic enough to attend sociable events in the evening. I asked Jennifer if this report were true. "Oh, yes," she replied. "But I like being home. Besides I am too weary at night to go out".

I knew that she had been checked out by the family physician and that there was nothing medically wrong. Anyone talking with her could see that she was mentally and emotionally stable. Most of her friends envied her. Seemingly she had everything, and yet something was wrong. What was it? Inwardly I questioned, hoped for answers, and silently prayed. It was a warm day, but I began to shiver as I felt a cold chill in the room. I glanced over at Jennifer and suddenly I received a strong impression of something or someone hovering over her! Unaccustomed to ghostly presences, I was startled. The unexpectedness of it was alarming. I shivered again. There was a dead silence in the room.

A few moments later, regaining my composure, I attempted to

question Jennifer again.

"How old were you when your mother died?"

"Fifteen."

"You were very close, very devoted to your mother?"

"Yes."

"You never talk about her, do you?"

"No."

"Do you have any pictures of her?"

"No."

"Do you mind my questions?"

Pause. "Yes."

"Is it hurtful?"

"No"

The answers came coldly polite as now I was intruding. The private person in Jennifer was saying, "I don't talk about things like that. Please stop." I was up against a stone wall and could go no further without breaking the law of non-interference and my adherence to the rule.

I stood up to leave, for now Jennifer really looked weary and spent, and I knew she would take her afternoon rest the moment I left. I sensed that she was in deeper trouble than either she or Emily or her husband could ever believe. One thing I could tell her that would be within the confines of the unbreakable law, and on that point I could speak with confidence. "Jennifer, dear, you do need help. There is something wrong. You sense it and that is why you agreed to my coming here. I believe there is help for you". Briefly her eyes lit up. "But first, Jennifer dear, you have to open the door of your heart and be willing to talk about your mother". She looked startled. "Think about it and let me know what you decide".

On the way home I wondered about that hovering I sensed. Was it the mother still clinging to her favorite beloved child, unable to let go? Was Jennifer unknowingly keeping her mother locked up? Did the mother originally gravitate in the direction of her strongest desire, her greatest attachment, only to become victimized by her own desires? Was Jennifer's lassitude caused by the presence of the dead? I knew from everything I had ever experienced that in order for the dead to stay close by the living, the vital energy of the living is consumed.

This was not possession, of that I was quite certain. A possessed person is usually completely taken over by another personality, loses her own identity, and displays behavior patterns strange, foreign and often destructive. In Jennifer's case everything except her unusual enervation was perfectly normal. Some call this "obsession" which more accurately explains that hovering like a cowl over Jennifer's head which I sensed The evidence of a devoted mother trying to shield her child, mistakenly thinking that by so doing, she is protecting her daughter.

I understood the problem better after my next visit with Jennifer, for she decided to unlock the door. It was a few days later that we met again. I will never know what prompted Jennifer to reveal herself after all the years of suppression, but I was happy for her that she made the decision without coercion on my part. She later explained that something inexplicable urged her on. Besides, her constant fatigue was getting worse daily and she was more desperate than any of us ever thought. She was weary of pretending that she was all right, weary of the cover-up. The timing was perfect, for I had approached her just when she had reached her lowest ebb.

Now she spoke freely about her mother. She talked of the strong bond between them. She adored her mother, and many times preferred to be with her rather than with her playmates. I got the impression, also verified by Emily, that the mother ruled the family, husband, daughters and son, with a powerful but loving hand. Her word was law and no one rebelled. When she became ill and knew that her disease was terminal, she fought it with every ounce of her strong will.

When the disease was first diagnosed, Jennifer was eleven years old. She remembered fighting tooth and nail against facing the truth, the inevitability of death from that dreaded disease cancer. As difficult as it was for Jennifer to accept, it was more difficult for the mother who customarily used her strong will to overcome all obstacles. When she finally passed on after dreadful suffering, Jennifer automatically suppressed her true feelings of grief, which then and there went underground.

Now, for the first time in fifteen years, her feelings of grief were allowed to surface. The dam was broken. She talked freely about all aspects of her childhood. She recalled funny little incidents as well as significant ones. We laughed and we cried, and inwardly I rejoiced, for I knew that Jennifer now was on the road to recovery.

And yet I had to be certain that her mother was free on the other side of life, so I asked and received permission 'to look on the inside' to see if all the ties had been cut and if her mother needed help. This could be determined by the inner work which I had always done in similar situations. If my suspicions about her mother's presence were correct, then it was of utmost importance that the tie between them be severed. Otherwise Jennifer's physical condition, bad as it was now, could only worsen with the years. Opening up and talking about her repressed feelings was not enough. She had to be free on every level in order to be released and restored to normal.

We would have to probe deeper, in the way I had been taught, in order to be certain that Jennifer's dead mother was the possible cause of Jennifer's abnormal inertia. And another unforeseen difficulty arose which indicated that the inner work was necessary to solve the problem.

As I was about to leave, Jennifer's little daughter Mary, a child of about five, came unexpectedly into the room. I had never met her before. She too was very pretty, but there was something strange about her. She walked into the room with an awkward gait. Her step was heavy. Her eyes were a hundred years old. She looked shyly at me, clutched at her mother's dress, and awkwardly climbed into her lap, promptly putting her thumb into her mouth. She was large for her age, and it was pathetic to see her try to curl up in her mother's lap like a baby, as though attempting to assume the foetal position. She stared at me out of her large dull brown eyes.

My heart ached for Jennifer. She looked so embarrassed and upset. I talked to little Mary and somehow, I really don't know how it happened, she responded. Perhaps it was because I told her that she reminded me of my own daughter at that age, and except for the expression in her large brown eyes, she did resemble my daughter. That did it. Mary wanted to know all about my little girl, and before I knew it we were conversing like two equals. I loved her there and then and she knew it.

Jennifer was stunned and later told me that never had she seen little Mary open up that way to a stranger. It was getting late, but before I left I promised Jennifer that I would meditate and work on her particular problem. We arranged for another meeting, for now we had to talk about Mary too.

Before the next session with Jennifer I checked on the inner level as I had promised. On the inner level I somehow 'knew' Jennifer's mother as soon as she appeared in front of my mental screen. She was walking away from some kind of an old structure, and passed directly in front of me. She merely glanced in my direction as she walked slowly and rather heavily in the opposite direction from the structure.

Something about her walk reminded me of someone, but I didn't stop to probe. The picture moved on. I saw to the right of me a glorious stream of light. The mother figure was hesitantly moving in that direction. Again she looked at me. I lifted my arm and pointed the way to that bright stream of light — nothing more — just pointed the way. "Keep it simple". I recalled the early instructions. This was utter simplicity. I watched until she merged with the Light. She was safe home at last! Never before or since had so little been done for so much to have been accomplished. I thanked the Almighty for giving me the privilege of serving and waited to be shown the next step.

I didn't have to wait long. A week after the session Jennifer called. I hardly recognized her voice. She was incredibly excited and elated. "What has happened to me?" were her first words". "I feel so great! You said that I would be helped, but I never expected anything like this. I am alive! I want to do things! I can't believe it's me, Jennifer. Wait until you hear from my husband. He doesn't know what to make of me. He is so thrilled. What is it all about? What was done? Whatever it was, whatever was done, it worked".

I told her that on the inner level I had found, as I had suspected, that her mother was 'earth-bound' and that she had been released. I explained as best I could the nature of the work, and a little about the importance of helping the dead release their hold on the living. I even told her of the strange, chilling experience I had on that day of my first visit with her.

Jennifer listened intently. "Is my mother all right now?" 1 reassured her that her mother indicated by her reactions that she wanted to be rescued, and I felt that she too was happier now.

I did hear from Jennifer's husband Jim. Although somewhat bewildered, he too was excited. "I am so thrilled," he cried, "Jennifer is so changed! What is the magic formula? She is setting new goals for herself, and is even starting tennis lessons. I can't believe it is my wife. And you can't even begin to know how happy I am". He thanked me profusely. Inwardly I thanked the Almighty and the inner teacher, for it was spiritual work that I was doing, following the teachings, trusting and believing that what I was led to do was constructive and right.

Now more than ever Jennifer wanted to talk about little Mary. She was deeply concerned and anxious to see if there was any kind of help for her daughter. Jennifer's willingness to reveal intimate problems was incredible. For someone accustomed to suppressing anything and everything unpleasant, she was unbelievably frank and articulate. In such a brief period she had changed.

From infancy Mary was difficult. As she grew older she exhibited strange and unpleasant traits. What I had witnessed that first day was a demonstration of her usual desire to become an infant cuddled in her mother's lap. She was belligerent and unhappy.

But most mystifying of all to Jennifer and other members of the family, was Mary's strange pre-occupation with her dead "Grandma Nell," as she called her. This was mystifying, because Jennifer never spoke about her mother, there were no photographs displayed anywhere. Except for an aunt, the mother's sister, who visited often and occasionally made a reference to her dead sister Nell, there was no reason for Mary to be so involved with someone she never knew. When Mary was naughty she would taunt her mother by proclaiming that Grandma Nell disapproved of such treatment of her little darling granddaughter. She would even tease her other living Grandmother by telling her that she loved Grandma Nell best. It was Grandma Nell this and Grandma Nell that, constantly.

It was a great puzzle to Jennifer. She usually avoided any rebuttal and walked away from a confrontation of the problem. She didn't know what to do or say, so she did nothing. "All in all," Jennifer concluded, "Jim and I believe that Mary is our cross to bear. We have everything else. Everyone has some sorrow in their lives. Why should we be exempt? We shall have to put her in some special school for problem children".

As the story unfolded I speculated. Did Mary come into the world afflicted with abnormal traits? Her kind of behavior pattern was not too uncommon. Were Jennifer and Jim right in giving up, believing that this was their "cross to bear?" Or was it something else? Could it be possible that Grandma Nell had also been affecting her grandchild? I voiced my suspicions to Jennifer; she grasped at the straw, wanting to believe. I cautioned her against jumping to any conclusions. There was little more that we could do at this time besides meditate, pray, and wait for developments.

But in my own mind I was fairly certain that not only had Jennifer been victimized by her mother, but also the next in line, Mary. At first it was only Jennifer's energy that was being drained, but as the years rolled by and as she became increasingly enervated, the earth-bound mother unwittingly began to absorb the natural energy, the normal life-force of her granddaughter.

Again, it has to be emphasized and cannot be stressed enough, in order for the dead to continue in the earth-bound condition they draw on the energy of the living. The ones they love most, victimized by the involvement, suffer physically and emotionally. Even though it appears to be malevolent and in the final analysis is destructive, the dead are not aware of this fact, and by the time they do become aware they can't do anything about it. It is too late. They are magnetically bound. As for the living victims, they are unaware of the real cause for their nervousness, sleeplessness, and general debilitation. With few exceptions, when so bound together, them living and the dead suffer. Jennifer's mother had crossed over to the other side of life still clinging to the daughter she loved and adored, still desirous of remaining close by rather than going on to her own destiny. She had crossed over to the other side of life without any preparation or knowledge of what to expect and do. What was initiated by her own strong will, motivated by possessive love and devotion, had gradually become a tie too strong for her alone to break. She had become hopelessly hooked into a situation harmful to the one she loved most. She didn't understand her predicament; she only knew that she was trapped. At long last, weary of her fight to stay close to Jennifer and later to

Mary, she yearned for her freedom and theirs.

By the time I came on the scene Jennifer's mother, Grandma Nell, was desperate, more than ready and most eager and willing to co-operate. Maybe she telepathically sent me a message that first day when I met with Jennifer. Maybe the chill I felt that day, the hovering presence, was her way of communicating with me and pleading for help. Perhaps she knew more than I that the time had come for her rescue; the person had come who could help. For if she had not been present in that strange, ghostly way, I would not have been alerted to the nature of Jennifer's and Mary's dilemma. Presences like this were quite alien to me. Now, nine years and many more experiences later, I realize the validity of the strange sequence of events and have grown somewhat accustomed to them. For the results were incredibly decisive, positive, and miraculous.

Within a matter of weeks Jennifer's youthful energy was completely restored, never to be diminished over the years. To this very day, nine years later, she leads an extremely active life. Anyone observing her daily schedule, her skills at tennis, her ability to run a large household efficiently, her involvement with community affairs, could never believe that this is the same lackadaisical, enervated young woman who caused her sister Emily so much worry and concern.

As miraculous as the change was in Jennifer, it was even more so in little Mary. Although the improvement was gradual, the results were even more extraordinary. The first things we all noticed were her posture, her walk, and her bright clear eyes. A few months after the release, Jennifer, Emily and I met to discuss all the remarkable changes in Mary. Jennifer was bubbling. "Did you expect such a change in Mary? I can't believe what I am witnessing. My child is so different! She no longer sucks her thumb or climbs into my lap. She looks, acts, and talks differently. She is no longer feisty. She is adorable — a complete joy". It was a thrilling moment for all of us.

I asked one more question. "Does she mention Grandma Nell anymore?"

"Why no, not at all now," Jennifer responded. "I was so excited about all the other changes that I didn't notice that change too. It is significant, isn't it?"

"Yes," I replied, "everything is significant. All the character improvements, all the physical changes, all that talk about Grandma Nell — all prove that our suspicions were correct that Mary too had been victimized".

Again, as so many times before with other cases, Jennifer's continued improvement, the return of her energy, and Mary's complete and total metamorphosis became convincing evidence of the effects of the work. And, of course, Jennifer was completely won over — completely certain. She accepted wholeheartedly the entire process, for now she knew by her own experience that there was another dimension of life — that the dead don't die but simply shed the physical body prior to assuming another way of life. Now she knew that the dead are often "earth-bound," encompassing the lives of the living. Now she knew that the living can help release the dead from bondage.

As for Jim, his initial enthusiasm gave way to skepticism. When Jennifer tried to explain how she had been helped, he resisted all discussion of anything bordering on the supernatural. A magic formula, a pill, a new kind of potion, anything would have been acceptable to him except a cure based on the belief that the dead can influence the living. A prosaic, down-to-earth businessman like Jim could not accept the mystical process, the unscientific approach. He was aware of the complete transformation in Jennifer and Mary, but he could not give credence to a remedy based on the belief of a life after death. He couldn't understand it, so he reasoned that it might have happened by chance or luck or that Mary perhaps had outgrown her defects. He rationalized. It was more comfortable for him, and although he was pleased and grateful, he preferred not to think about it. It was too mystical — too far-out. Like many others, what he couldn't understand, he turned away from and rejected.

Jennifer and I understood his position and never tried to convince him of the truth as we had experienced it. Perhaps we were wrong, but I do not believe in forcing my opinions on others and couldn't bring myself to argue with Jim, or with anyone else. It was enough that Jennifer had complete acceptance and understanding of the miracle of the release. For Jennifer did accept wholeheartedly the entire process and benefitted enormously not only by experiencing the extra-ordinary transformation in herself and Mary, but also, more importantly, by becoming aware of the spiritual quality of life. It has broadened her outlook on daily living and gives her a much deeper appreciation of the gift of life. She studies spiritual laws, she meditates, and she works with me in helping others in a similar predicament. In the midst of a very busy schedule she never turns down an opportunity to serve others as she has been served, and by so doing she is obeying one of the great laws of the universe — the law of receiving and giving to life.

Although Jim was a beneficiary, it was Jennifer's lesson, not his. So I rationalized and willingly abandoned all thoughts of convincing Jim, and others like Jim. Jennifer and I agreed that we would not and could not impose unwanted knowledge upon Jim. However, fate had other plans in store for us. A few years later Jim, Jennifer and I were destined to become involved in one of the most bizarre situations of all my many experiences.

Nothing in this world is so marvellous as the transformation that a soul undergoes when the light of faith descends upon the light of reason.

W. Bernard Ullathorne
— *Endowments of Man*

Chapter 7

Jim Senior and Jim Junior

Jim's batteries were overcharged. He ran numerous enterprises with high-voltage energy and worked at such a speed his associates often complained that it was impossible to keep up with him. Jennifer was very worried about him and many times remarked to me that she did not know how much longer he could keep going without a serious collapse. To offset his frenzied business activities, she travelled often with him — just to get him away from the office. On pleasure trips he was always much better and she felt if he could manage more vacation periods, he would survive.

As time went on he seemed to get worse, even on vacations. Never a good sleeper, his inability to have a normal night's rest was becoming a real problem. He rarely got more than a few hours of fitful sleep, and spent most of the night pacing the floor, writing notes on how to conduct some new business venture, thinking and planning but not sleeping.

At first I thought this was a familiar pattern of many successful men who seem to drive themselves to the limit of their endurance until they either suffer an ulcer or a heart attack — it is the American businessman syndrome. I hoped that would not happen to Jim as I was very fond of him. He was such a good, kind man.

I knew that his father had died suddenly when Jim was three years old. Even though he manifested traits common to those who are tied to the dead, I wasn't about to conclude that an over-rought, harrassed businessman was obsessed by a dead father! Besides, I reasoned, the experience with Jennifer and Mary was enough for one family.

But as time went on, his condition worsened and I began to suspect it could be possible that Jim also was obsessed. I cautiously voiced my suspicion to Jennifer who immediately seized upon the suggestion as a possibility. But how could we approach Jim, of all people, with this idea? He had never understood or accepted the method which so dramatically released Jennifer and Mary. And after all these years he had even forgotten their former condition. Somehow, the timing wasn't quite right. Maybe we had to have more evidence. As we waited I advised Jennifer to watch for any changes, any event, any condition, even a dream — some sign that would indicate that Jim would be desperate enough, and hence more receptive to our kind of help.

If one really watches carefully and lets life events show the way, one can be led in the right direction at the right time. Fully a year after our suspicions were voiced, not only did Jim's condition worsen, but the youngest son, Dick, became a problem. At ten years of age Dick was irresponsible, strangely absent-minded, and given to imaginary day-dreaming. He not only fantasized, but fully believed his stories. He couldn't understand his punishments for fantasizing or forgetfulness because he was not aware that he had done any thing wrong.

Many other strange behavior patterns had developed insidiously over the last few years. Again, it was so reminiscent of his sister Mary that we hesitated to give credence to a similar cause. But when Jim was rushed to the hospital with chest pains and Dick was having serious problems in school, I thought, this is the sign — perhaps the signal that we had been waiting for all these months. Something must be done.

I was galvanized into action. The least I could do was either to investigate the possibility of obsession by a dead father or eliminate it altogether. First I had to overcome my own reluctance to accept a situation so fraught with weird coincidences. A situation in the same family so similar to Jennifer's problem and Mary's condition was incredibly strange and almost beyond belief. Secondly I had to deal with my sensitivity to Jim's increasing disapproval of my relationship with Jennifer. He was too kind a person to openly offend me, but in many subtle ways I sensed his feelings. He loved his wife and went along with anything that would make her happy, and so he reluctantly accepted our relationship. As Jennifer never let her outside activities interfere with her duties at home and was so completely devoted to him, he never complained.

I would have preferred to continue to remain in the background as I had for the past few years, but now I was forced to overcome my personal unwillingness to face Jim's hostility. He was in a distressful situation fraught with disaster. There must be no place in my heart for the hurt vanity of the personality. My inner self, the real Self, knew that the time had come to cast aside all personal feelings in order to try to rescue an endangered human being.

Jim was completely unaware of the nature of his predicament. Having discouraged any effort on our part to enlighten him when Jennifer and Mary were restored to normalcy, he could not benefit now from their experience. Any discussion with him about the situation and our suspicions of its cause were out of the question — an impossible consideration. Now the problem was not *whether* to help Jim, but *how*.

Fortunately Jim's mother, Martha, was still alive. She believed in meditation, had worked with me many times and knew the nature of the method. She is a rare wonderful person, deeply spiritual and dedicated to the principle of service to others. Besides our mutual interest, we are very close and devoted friends. I knew that her first husband, Jim Snr, had died suddenly in an automobile accident about thirty-eight years ago. Although Martha had recently recuperated from a serious operation, I hoped she would be sufficiently restored to health so that I could discuss with her the details of the death of her husband, Jim's father. Looking for guidelines on how to proceed, I hoped that a review of the early years of Martha's life would supply the clue.

Martha lived in another city, but when I called her immediately she suggested that we meet because she had something of vital importance to discuss with me. We arranged an appointment for the very next day. If it were at all possible, she seemed more anxious for the meeting than I, and for very good reason. She greeted me with great emotion, "I was just about to call you when your call came through. Isn't that just like us?" she queried. "We always seem to know when one of us is in distress". Mental telepathy between good friends. "Would you mind," she asked, "if I speak my piece first as I am so terribly worried?"

I agreed, inwardly knowing that she was going to talk about Jim Jnr. And of course that was it. She, too, had been aware for a long time that her son was abnormally overactive and frenetic, but lately he seemed worse than ever. She had always thought that Jim was driving himself far beyond normal physical endurance and had often spoken about it to Jennifer and me. But she, too, reasoned that many successful businessmen are similarly compelled.

"I don't want to seem like an overly solicitous motherhen," she said, "but there is something so unnatural about Jim's frenzied behavior, I am fearful for his very life". The tears flowed. "I don't like the way he acts or the way he looks. It is getting worse all the time. I don't see how he can go on this way much longer. He is *driven!*"

She had voiced my concern and Jennifer's deep fears. I told Martha that this problem was the reason for my call. She brightened. "I feel better already," she said. "Sharing my apprehensions with you has given me comfort and hope".

She had great faith in our method as she had studied and worked with it for years and knew from her own experience the benefits. It's easier to work with someone of her background and training in esoteric studies than with someone ignorant of the basic principles of spiritual truths. She believed and accepted wholeheartedly the continuity of life and the thin veil separating the visible and invisible world. I cautioned her that in order to help her son she would have to revive old memories of a very painful past event.

Although apprehensive, she was more than willing. She was eager and impatient to begin immediately, and proceeded to give me a detailed account of the most traumatic experience of her life. As her extraordinary story unfolded and the evidence mounted, I began to believe we were on the right track.

In many ways Jim Jnr was very much like his dad. Jim Snr was also a brilliant operator and by the time he was twenty-five years old he was already a success — in his own way he was a genius. He and Martha were deeply in love and both adored their little son.

One evening as Martha was preparing dinner she answered the phone and was informed by the police that her husband had just been killed in an automobile accident. Her world came to an end. With no warning she was catapulted from a life of joy and promise to a life of emptiness and grief. She was inconsolable until one night shortly after her husband's untimely death, he appeared before her. She felt his arms around her, soothing and comforting her with familiar words of love and devotion. At first she was startled and shocked by this experience but as time went on she grew accustomed to the presence and found great comfort in this new, though strange, relationship.

The nightly visitations eased her anguish and made her empty days tolerable. And he never disappointed her! He was always there — always communicating his thoughts and feelings — always reassuring her of his undying love for her!

Martha's life now assumed a definite pattern of ordinary daily activities and unusual nightly communication with her dead husband. The days were full of meetings with attorneys for the estate and attempts to carve out some kind of life for herself and little Jim, the nights were spent in this unnatural relationship.

Martha, gregarious and outgoing, was popular and admired by both sexes. Before the year was up she was occasionally invited by one of her numerous friends to a dinner party with some eligible male escort. She would return home at night, walk into her bed room and find Jim there waiting for her. Wildly jealous, protesting vigorously, he would make her promise never again to accept these invitations.

Martha began to dread the nights and Jim's possessiveness. As time went on, his presence became increasingly irksome to her. The altercations between them grew more irritating and unbearable. For now Jim Snr fearful of losing his hold on her, hovered around her during the day as well as the night! Their inner conversations never ceased. He became more and more demanding of her time and energy. "I would be talking to someone, anyone," she said, "and at the same time Jim and I would be inwardly conversing. He never for one minute left me alone!"

It was maddening and she literally thought she was going out of her mind. What had begun as a comfort became an intolerable burden. Although an emotionally and mentally stable woman, Martha feared for her sanity and yearned for a return to normalcy. As much as she had loved Jim, she could no longer tolerate his constant presence — could no longer endure the sleepless nights, the continuous haranguing. She became exceedingly nervous and irritable, but fearful of being mis-understood and ridiculed, confided in no one. She barely functioned during the day, and dreaded even more the agony of the nights.

As time went on the tension between Martha and Jim mounted and became so excruciatingly painful that one night in desperation she cried out to him hysterically, "Go away! Leave me alone. I have to take care of our son. I can't go on this way any longer! If you ever loved me, go now and let me live my own life. There is no other way. Go!... please go". She sobbed out her anguish.

There was no reply. The room was filled with the silence. No protestations, no arguments — silence. She cried herself to sleep and awoke the following morning with a strange feeling of emptiness — emptiness and relief. And now, after thirty-eight years of welcome silence, I was about to ask Martha to revive the contact!

During those years she had happily remarried, had had other children, and lived a normal active life, the trauma of the past buried deep in her memory. We discussed her emotional state the night of her last conversation with Jim.

"If he hadn't obeyed my command that night," she exclaimed, "I would have committed myself to an institution for the mentally ill. No one can ever tell me that death is the end. I *know* that there is a survival of the person. I *know* that Jim was with me for two years. When I first heard about life after death and the earth-bound, I knew from my own experience that the entire concept is true. But isn't it strange," she went on, "that the moment I screamed at him, Jim left me and has never come back?"

Cautiously I questioned her. "Are you certain of that? Can we be certain?"

We sat together silently. I wondered how much more she could tolerate and if now was the appropriate time to tell her that I suspected that Jim Snr was still earth-bound, had left her only to attach himself to his son, living out his interrupted career in the life of Jim Jnr! Although Jim Snr's physical body had been shed, the drive for power was still alive, increasing daily in its insatiable desire for expression, paralyzing father and son into submission — the power now dominating both the living and the dead.

An awareness of the underlying problem opens the way to a solution, and now I knew what had to be done. "Yes, Martha, there is something we can do. Jim did leave you that fateful night, but he did not leave the material world. He left you and then attached himself to his son. Now we must correct that mistake.

He obeyed your command and could have gone on to his rightful place on the other side of life, but he chose to remain on earth. He could have been helped had you known how and what to do. Although you were right in ordering your husband to leave, we have learned that the dead sometimes need further instructions. They have to be told where to go, what is in store for them. They have to be told about the Light on their path."

"Can't Jim order his father to leave him, just as I did?"

It was a valid suggestion, and under ordinary circumstances the obvious solution. But tell Jim Jnr that? Jim Jnr who rejects all such ideas? For the first time we laughed as we tried to imagine Jim Jnr engaged in such a project! — Jim Jnr talking to his dead father and showing him the way to heaven! It was funny and broke us up for a moment....

Our laughter subsided and we became serious again. "Then what are we going to do?" Martha wanted to know. "I don't think Jim can take it much longer. I know he is reaching the end of his endurance! There must be something?"

"Yes, Martha," I replied, "there is something that can be done if you think you are strong enough. Even though many years have elapsed, you and you only have the right to call upon your husband and correct the error".

"Of course, I will do anything you suggest — anything — I must — I want to and the sooner the better".

It was settled and we agreed to meet in three days, meanwhile utilizing the intervening time for preparation which involved a special kind of meditation. Martha was given a specific symbol for meditation, a symbol often used in preparation for separating the living and the dead. It is a concise and specific symbol. Martha was instructed to visualize a circle of light completely surrounding her dead husband. Similarly she had to visualize her son in another circle of light. Each one was placed in his own orbit — two circles side by side, separate but touching at one point — much like a figure of eight.[1] This was fairly simple for Martha since she was accustomed to meditating daily.

A few days later we met again. Our meditations had given us strength and had shown a definite direction to follow. Martha, visibly nervous and slightly apprehensive, questioned her ability to control her emotions if after all these long years she had to acknowledge the presence of Jim Snr again. I reassured her and told her that in all our experiences we were always stunned by the utter simplicity of the process and impressed by the comparative ease in which so much resulted from such a seemingly uncomplicated method. According to my meditations of the past three days, all that was required of her were her preparatory meditations, her prayers, and her presence. Somehow, together we had to communicate with Jim Snr. He did not know me and it would be simpler if she were present.

We began. We prayed together. I deliberately called out many times to Jim Snr, firmly and authoritatively. When we 'felt' his presence I proceeded to converse with him as though he were really physically with us.

Because I never doubted that such a thing was possible, I had no trouble communicating with him. I told him that Martha and I had come to help him. Relating the complete circumstances of his sudden death thirty-eight years ago, I explained that he no longer had a physical body, that without a physical body life on earth was frustrating and impossible. Further, that he had been using the life energy of his son in order to fulfill his own ambition, and that this was destructive. I warned him that his son was on the verge of a serious collapse.

Martha remained calm and in silent prayer during the entire session.

Jim seemed to listen as though he knew as well as we did the reason for this meeting. When we informed him of his present condition and the problems it was causing, it was incredible how swiftly he capitulated. Martha was not traumatized by the meeting. She was 'uplifted', particularly when she witnessed his definite willingness to co-operate.

Upon our suggestion he made a complete turnabout in the opposite direction. Instead of whirling frantically in the earth's atmosphere, unconscious of his condition, unconscious of his destructiveness to himself and those closest to him, he obeyed and followed our directions, understanding telepathically. When he finally became aware of the Light leading him up and beyond, there was no more hesitancy. And when last we were aware of him, he was being guided on his return path — home to God.

To describe in words something that has to be experienced is almost impossible. There are no words that can adequately convey the full impact of such a confrontation. Words become sacrilegious and detract from the awesome quality of such experiences. The entire process took about an hour — an hour in which Martha and I were transported into another dimension of the mind. Fully conscious of our own material world, we were at the same time participating in another world outside of our time and place. Though strange and unusual for both of us, it was never for one moment uncomfortable or awkward. Instead, there was a simple reality about it that was convincingly true.

Again, the only proof that would be persuasive rested on the results — the effects on the living. Subsequent events again proved beyond a shadow of a doubt that Jim Snr had vacated the premises, as it were. By so doing he gave his son the opportunity of being his own person, and his grandson the right to grow up normally — both free from hostile influences.

Almost immediately after the session with Martha, Jim showed remarkable improvement. For the first time in years he slept the night through without sedation. The very next morning after our work and Jim's first night of sound rest, he commented upon that unusual event with joy and amazement. As this pattern of nocturnal rest repeated itself every night, he kept exclaiming to Jennifer, "I really slept again last night! I don't know what's happened to me. I feel great! I'm a new man". Over and over again he repeated the words, "a new man" or "the new Jim." Over and over again he remarked how different he felt, how relaxed. His office personnel and friends commented on the change and expressed amazement at the 'improved' Jim. After thirty days of continuous glowing reports we all accepted that the work had passed the test of time, and that Jim was no longer in desperate trouble.

As the months went by Jim continued to improve in other unexpected ways. Not only was he calmer and unfrenzied, but his attitude toward Martha changed considerably. We had all been so concerned for his physical survival, and so relieved when that was no longer crucial, that we didn't look for other developments. But there were other extraordinary changes that were equally significant. For years Martha had been aware of her son's belligerent and some times hostile attitude toward her. Believing that in some way she had failed him when he was growing up, she blamed herself.

Jim, on the other hand, couldn't understand why his mother aroused such antagonism in him. He confessed many times to Jennifer that he couldn't account for the fact that whenever he was in his mother's company, some deep resentment was triggered off in him which made him caustic and sharp with her. Whenever they were together the sparks flew.

I recall Martha once telling me that when Jim was a little boy she would return home from a date and be greeted angrily by her young son. On those occasions it was the accusing look in his eyes which frightened her. As the young child grew to manhood the accusing eyes were accompanied by an intensely disapproving attitude toward her. As adults, even though loving and caring for each other, try as they both did they could not overcome this unnatural belligerence. And now, suddenly, as though by magic, that feeling of antagonism between them was gone. Free from antagonism and resentment, Jim was able to express normal love for his mother. In the Bright Light of life beyond death, unnatural antagonisms and resentments dissipate and cease to exist.

All this was proof that our efforts were successful. Nothing else could account for Jim's improved health, his calmer attitude toward life in general, and his pleasant, relaxed change of attitude toward his mother. It was there for all to see — there for Jennifer, Martha and me to know how and why. The added plus for all of us, not to be minimized, was little Dick's gradual return to normal behavior. He is achieving an outstanding record in school, and no longer manifests the odd traits which caused so many problems. Now the real person is in evidence — well adjusted and extraordinarily intelligent.

Martha and I left it up to Jennifer how much and what to tell Jim. She tried to explain to him the reason for his metamorphosis and Dick's improvement. She casually mentioned that a special kind of meditation had been engaged in by his mother. Jim refused to listen, his mind still closed to any suggestion other than what conformed to established concepts.

In a way it is regrettable that Jim was not open to the kind of efforts made in his behalf and the true reason for his improvement. A healing of this nature is a high spiritual experience, and know-ledge of a life after death gained by a personal involvement greatly enhances the understanding of life in the here and now. Jim's type of experience usually brings a deeper understanding of the purpose of life, a broadened view of the eternal process, a joy in living, a gratitude for life. I am sorry that Jim could not experience the full benefit of his improved condition. Although Jennifer tried many times to broach the subject, Jim would have none of it. He wasn't ready for that kind of enlightenment. Maybe at some future time his mind will be more open.

Although it is regrettable that Jim remained ignorant of the cause of his renewed health and equanimity, on the other hand, the success of the work could never be attributed to suggestibility. A closed mind like Jim's is barren soil for the sowing of the seeds of suggestion. Jim's spiritually oriented mother had saved him and restored him to a life of normal activity. For the time being, we had to be satisfied and grateful for what had been accomplished. We could not penetrate the wall of resistance — the closed mind.

Renounce all fruit of action. Thy
business is with the action only,
never with the fruits; so let not the
fruit of action be thy motive, nor
be thou to inaction attached.

— *The Bhagavad Gita*

Chapter 8

Sudden Death

Contrary to popular belief the most harrowing and difficult way to make the final exit from earthly existence is to leave suddenly without warning. One moment the person is moving about in his physical body, and the next he is unceremoniously jolted out of his familiar surroundings, his patterned existence, into a strange condition. He is bodiless, and yet he thinks and feels! He sees and hears what is going on in his environment, but he cannot converse with those whom he senses all around him. He feels weightless, incredibly light, free of his heavy physical body, and yet in all other respects he is much the same, very much alive. No one around him answers him when he 'speaks,' and no one responds to him when he touches them. What is the matter with everybody? Why all the fuss, he thinks. He looks down and 'sees' his physical body and wonders what is wrong, why the weeping. He is confused and completely bewildered!

And is it any wonder! Having been carefully indoctrinated by the belief that death is the end, or at best an eternal sleep, he doesn't understand his new status. Having accepted the finality of death, having stubbornly refused to harbor any other belief, he is totally unprepared for the frustrating and bewildering experience of that moment when the silver cord is cut and his life in the physical body terminated. No wonder English churchmen are taught to pray, "From battle, murder and sudden death, Good Lord, deliver us".

For every other journey we make careful preparation. We decide on our destination — perhaps a trip to Paris or London. We purchase the tickets, consult with travel agents, book our reservations in hotels of our choice, buy the proper clothes, and pack our suitcases. We wouldn't care to take any trip abroad, or even in our own country, without some kind of planning. The more important the journey, the more trouble we take to work out every detail. Most of us would not even travel in our own cities into an unknown area without consulting a city map or asking of the nearest gasoline attendant explicit directions.

Yet for the most important journey of our entire lives, we make incomplete provisions. Certainly, if we are wise, we will make a will properly signed, pick out a plot in the cemetery grounds, or arrange for cremation. This we do routinely, mistakenly thinking that we have taken care of everything. And as far as it goes, that much preparation is basically essential. But have we considered other possibilities — the possibility of conscious survival of the Self.

Have we thoroughly investigated and weighed the evidence — claimed by great minds and profound thinkers throughout the centuries? Have we read the words on this subject of a Walt Whitman, a Tennyson, a Wordsworth, or a Dante? Have we considered the philosophy of Ouspensky, Emerson, Plato, Bucke and countless others? Have we listened to Tennyson who proclaims of death that it is a "laughable impossibility?" And what about the millions of followers of Eastern religions whose faith is grounded in the belief of a life after death, and Christians who subscribe to the belief of the resurrection?

Why delay in fear and trembling the search for truth and understanding? The more we familiarize ourselves with all the available knowledge of this inevitable event, the more we alleviate the fear and the dread of the unknown. By discussing the varying points of view, accepting some and discarding others, we illuminate the dark corners of our minds. By throwing a little light on a much neglected subject, by probing and searching for answers, we begin to make the unknown known.

To those who die suddenly, totally oblivious to the possibility of survival, the shock is greater than the shock to those left behind! At least the survivor knows what has happened, but the victim of a sudden death, unprepared and ignorant of the process, is bewildered and panic stricken. Just as a little child, lost in a crowd, separated from its parents, becomes dreadfully frightened, so one taken abruptly from the physical Life stream is in desperate need of reassurance. But everyone around him is either trying to revive him or else hysterically immersed in their own grief. And so the lost child goes comfortless.

The phone rings and the voice on the other end informs me that a mutual friend has just passed away.

"I hate to be the bearer of such sad news," my friend says, "I know how much you loved Rosalie". Her voice breaks and we cry silently as we share our sense of loss. "How did it happen?" I ask.

"She and her husband, Bill, were just about to leave the house for an evening at the theater when she grew faint and died instantly. It was dreadful for Bill, but such a nice easy way for her to go. I hope it happens like that for me".

"Oh, no," I thought, "it is not really that good, not a happy state for a Rosalie."

Rosalie, the agnostic, had often expressed to me her opinion of death. I can hear her now proclaiming in no uncertain terms that "when you are dead, you are dead, finished". I recall how she had once picked up a small gray stone and holding it in the palm of her hand, firmly declared, "That's what we turn into, a little gray stone". And how she laughed in her own merry infectious way!

She was so certain, so sure of her convictions that she discouraged any discussion. Looking at me impishly she remarked that she knew I felt differently and thought it must be truly wonderful to have that kind of belief. Never one to argue, particularly on this subject, I suggested a reading list and concluded the conversation. After many rebuffs I have learned never to engage in a fruitless discussion with anyone with such set, rigid convictions. She didn't know how I had arrived at my conclusions, nor was she particularly curious. Her door was shut tightly! I knew from all that I had been taught that Rosalie was in trouble. Sudden death to the Rosalies of this world is one of the most difficult ways of departure. A short or even a long illness would have been preferable, in the long run, to crossing so abruptly the line from physical life to death in such ignorance. Painful as it is, an illness does serve the purpose of preparation. But a Rosalie suddenly catapulted into a new state of being without any landmarks, frantically trying to call attention to her aliveness, bewildered by her inability to make contact, never for one moment realizing that death has overtaken her — for a Rosalie such a state is unbelievable torture.

My friend Dee broke the silence. "Do you and your friends

say a special kind of prayer when someone passes on?" she asked, knowing something about the work in which I was involved. It was not idle curiosity that prompted the question, for she had been reading and studying about life after death and had recently come to the conclusion that death was not the end. I sensed that she was ready to participate actively in the kind of special prayer that a sudden death requires. I liked the idea that there would be more of us contacting Rosalie, for "where two or more are gathered" there is strength and power. Besides Dee, who was closest to Roslie, was the ideal person to join in our kind of prayer work. For years I had automatically prayed and communicated with sudden death victims, even before I was totally convinced, as I am today, that they benefitted. It was an inner prompting urged on by faith, now grounded in a strong conviction.

Dee asked for instructions on what to do. "Remember," I told her, "the newly dead are not very far removed in consciousness from the scene of their life's activity. First of all, call Rosalie by name and identify yourself".

"You mean," asked Dee, "that I should say, 'Rosalie, this is Dee' several times?"

"Yes, just like that. Remember she is disoriented and needs to get her bearings. Mentally visualize and think that she is in the room with you. Just hearing your words of identification is already a comfort to her. It is actually thought transference, mental telepathy. We convey our message in words because it is easier for us. The dead 'hear' the thoughts. It is in that sense that we communicate with them. After establishing your identity, tell her every minute detail of the way in which she died. Tell her everything you know, even what she was wearing. You know that she was going out to the theater, so tell her that. You know that her last words were, 'I feel dizzy.' Tell her that too".

Dee interrupted, "Will she answer me?"

"No," I answered. "We are not in trance. We are not mediums. We are friends believing there is a great need which we are serving in the way that has been taught — with a method that has proven to be effective. Just keep talking to her, believing in your heart that her anguish will be relieved. When you have established your identity and all the facts known to her, you must point the way out of her dilemma. Over and over again tell her about the Light. In your own words remind her of her parents whom she loved dearly and who will be on that path of Light. She has to be told in order to become aware of the Light and the presence of her parents. The Light is right there where she is, obscured only by her ignorance and denial of it. Once she opens up her heart and her mind, she will see it, and when she sees it, she will see everyone she loves who is on that side of Life. She will be royally welcomed".

Dee solemnly promised to follow the instructions, and I promised that my friends and I would join her. But I emphasized that her participation was important because she was much closer to Rosalie than any of us.

Dee called the next day, eager to tell me her experience. At first she reported that she felt awkward as she whispered Rosalie's name. She couldn't help wondering if the contact had really been made. "I know now what you mean by a 'prayer of faith'," she said. "But as I continued it became easier. I was concentrating so intently on giving Rosalie the exact description of her last moments, visualizing her presence, determined to include each and every detail as you had outlined for me, that I lost my self-consciousness and felt in some obscure way that Rosalie was really listening. And when I told Rosalie about the Light, a wonderful feeling of peace and awe over came me and I knew that what I was doing was good. l would never have believed praying like that for Rosalie so soon after her death could bring me such comfort. It relieved my own pain".

For several days after that Dee and I repeated the conversations and prayer work for Rosalie until we felt reasonably certain that she had the information which would allow her to make her own choice. For in the final analysis, we could only show the way — give her the key. But she had to open her own door!

No special training is required for anyone to 'talk' in this manner to the victims of sudden death. Nor does it matter whether or not one is completely convinced. The possibility that it may be true should be enough to induce anyone to make the attempt to help those who suddenly pass on and not abandon them in their great hour of need. Momentarily putting aside one's own grief, subordinating it to comfort the departed, is an act of love and kindness.

In a perfunctory survey which we made, most people indicated that if they were given choices they would prefer to die suddenly. If these same people had made sufficient inquiries into the nature of the death process, realizing the full meaning of that momentous event, knowing that the vacated lifeless physical body is their own discarded garment useless to them in their new environment, then they could safely make the transition from life into death, suddenly or any other way.

It is lack of knowledge of this natural occurrence in our lives which causes many to be confused and makes of the inevitable event a mysterious, fearful trauma. The informed person who has had some teaching on this subject and has learned what to expect, will be able to face the inevitable event of their lives secure in their understanding. Their knowledge enables them to cope with a sudden departure from life without fear or shock. Knowledge has its own way of shedding its light in the dark recesses of unknown, dreaded corridors.

The world recedes; it disappears!
Heav'n opens on my eyes! my ears
  With sounds seraphic ring!
Lend, lend your wings! I mount! I fly!
O Grave! where is thy victory?
  O Death! where is thy sting?

Alexander Pope
— *Vital Spark of Heavenly Flame*

Our birth is but a sleep and a forgetting:
The Soul that rises with us, our Life's Star,
Hath had elsewhere its setting,
And cometh from afar:
Not in entire forgetfulness,
And not in utter nakedness,
But trailing clouds of glory we do come
From God, who is our home.

Wordsworth — *Ode on Intimations of Immortality*

Chapter 9

The Earth-Bound

If the promise of happiness awaits the normal human being, then it is to be expected that those who have violently taken or contributed to the taking of another's life will not experience the same felicitous outcome. Although different religious traditions have painted graphic images of the fate that awaits the murderers and evil doers, it need not be our concern to imagine what kind of punishment awaits them. In the life review they will face, the shock of recognizing the suffering they have inflicted on others, often by obeying the orders of their leaders, may be enough to change their understanding and bring regret and remorse for what they have done. The law of justice prevails in these other dimensions — a law, however, mitigated by mercy. When true repentance takes place, much will be forgiven.

Our concern is not for those extremists, but for the average man or woman who may be far from perfect and struggles through life with its pains and pleasures as best he can. With rare exceptions the human record is just that — human — which indicates that man in the course of his life may at times experience or be taken over by hatred, resentment, anger, malice and greed. He may only be able with the greatest difficulty to free himself from these age-old patterns that are so much a part of the human condition and can often originate in childhood trauma. With help and insight he may be able to reach a more spiritually aware state of being.

Each lifetime is involved with this struggle and no one need fear that he will be condemned for his shortcomings. The respite which death offers will be given him regardless of his human imperfections. When the particular struggle of one life time is over and man steps into that other dimension of life which is beyond death, the release from the struggle, from the burden, is a welcome event. The feeling of buoyancy which he experiences when at long last has shed his physical body, perhaps after suffering a debilitating illness, brings him sheer joy and ecstasy. He sees the welcoming Light and is irresistibly drawn to it. He sees the Light and knows he is safe!

Average men and women should expect just that. We have countless numbers of reports from reliable individuals who, in relating their near-death experience (NDE), describe the feeling as buoyant, light, free. I recall the story of one of my closest friends who had been declared clinically dead for ten minutes. During that time she floated above and beyond her ill physical body. Traveling in another kind of body (often called the astral body) through the city of Berlin, recognizing landmarks, sensing the damp cold air, she could still 'see' the hospital room several miles away where the nurses and physicians were working over her body making a supreme effort to revive her. Light-headed and unconcerned for her sick physical body, detached from any feeling of fear or desire, she floated weightlessly and happily in another kind of dimension.

Later she reported to the doctors and nurses everything they had said and done during the time she had vacated her body. They confirmed the truth of her observation and remarked that it was not the first time a patient had revealed this type of experience to them. She summed it all up when she said to me, "If that is death, I have no fear of it, and I know that I will welcome it when my time is up. I felt so vibrant and alive in that other body!"

The serious problem is with those who pass on still clinging to their physical body, their desires, and their old life in the material world. In spite of all the hardships and heartaches of their past existence, they prefer to remain in the closeness of their familiar surroundings rather than go forward into the next experience. They disbelieve reports of the radiant Light, the joy and happiness which awaits them in the next dimension, and stubbornly cling to a mother, a child, a husband, a wife, or their material possessions. Refusing to accept their new status in the world beyond, stubbornly insisting upon having their own way, they deprive themselves of the far greater happiness which awaits them. The feeling of aliveness which typifies the condition of the person in that other dimension of life beyond death, deceives them into thinking that they have not really died, and so they hang around. They struggle to remain where they do not belong and often times are not even wanted.

These are the so-called "earth-bound" — rightly named for that condition which describes the departed who refuse to move on. Such people remain close to their old ways of existence, and cling to the physical earth where they no longer live. Belonging to neither world, they are homeless.

There is a great need to help not only the dead who are earth-bound but also the living who are victimized by their invisible presence. In releasing one or the other, both are saved; each one allowed to live his own life in his own world, unfettered by the desires and stubbornness of the other — free.

There are countless numbers of people who are completely unaware of the unseen presence of the earth-bound, and therefore are unable to cope with the problem. There are many, like Ella, Jennifer and Jim who suffer the debilitating effects without knowing the cause of their nervousness, sleeplessness, restlessness, or distress. These cases are more difficult to diagnose than those who directly experience the presence of the departed by some outward sign of action. Over the following pages I relate a number of such cases which will illustrate the greater ease of diagnosis.

LYDIA

There are many who have a clear indication of being obsessed and of times tormented by the activities of the dead. One such beleaguered woman, about fifty-five years of age, came to me several years ago with a not too uncommon problem. Shortly after her husband died she was awakened during the night by the feeling of someone in the room with her, shaking her to awaken her. Frightened by the thought that it seemed like her dead husband's touch, she turned on the light and tried to resume her interrupted sleep. Much to her distress this happening began to occur regularly.

Some months later she met another man who had lost his wife and finding they had much in common they began to spend a great deal of time together. Now the nightly interruptions of her dead husband began to take on a more ominous meaning. Lydia had heard about our work with the dead from a friend and had asked if she might come to see me. I liked her immediately. She was straight forward, sincere, and most pleasant. She explained her marriage by informing me that it had been like many marriages, "full of ups and downs" but on the whole quite satisfactory. Her newly found male friend was in many ways more congenial than her husband, and she was anxious to continue the relationship without being tormented by feelings of guilt. She didn't know what to do. She hated to give up the companionship which was making her life so pleasant and enjoyable and at the same time she was afraid of the disturbing presence of her dead husband.

"If my husband would leave me alone, I could be so happy. But at night, when I feel his finger nails digging into my shoulder, shaking me to awaken me, I wonder if he is trying to tell me something. There is no conversation or anything like that, for always when I turn on the light he goes away and I am alone again. I think perhaps my husband doesn't want me to be with another man, but I don't want to give up my friend. I am losing so much sleep over this and I don't know what to do". She was bewildered and frightened — her life made miserable by an occurrence which she had no way of controlling.

It was a dilemma. Lydia was locked into a predicament which seemed unsolvable. I reassured her that perhaps her dead husband did not object to the new relationship because he had begun his nightly visits to her long before she had met her present friend. She agreed, but couldn't understand why he had become so increasingly insistent, disturbing her sleep.

I suggested that he probably was earth-bound, wanted to go on, but couldn't make it without her help. "He is trying in the only way he knows to awaken you and make you aware of his need. There are some people who die without any preparation for the life beyond and somehow lose their way. That seems to be your husband's problem. There are countless numbers like him, but he is more fortunate than most of them because he has been able to contact you and make you aware of his dilemma. I believe he wants his freedom as much as you do".

Basing my premise on the assumption that this man had lost his way and was seeking help, I explained to Lydia the method that had been successfully used for similar cases. She gladly accepted the explanation and appeared relieved that there was a solution.

In retrospect I am completely amazed how readily most people responded and agreed to the unusual procedure. Lydia was no exception. With great trust she easily joined me in the prayer of release. The response from Lydia's husband was exceptionally good. Lydia herself was magnificent in her conversation with him as she explained the situation and his impossible status in trying to maintain a way of life inconsistent with his condition. She told him of the Bright Light and suggested he look for helpers to guide him to his new abode. She was reassuring as she tried to transmit to him her own belief that he would be much better off going on to where he belonged — the place that was right for him. We concluded as usual with the Twenty-third Psalm.

The results were instantaneous. From that moment on Lydia's dead husband never again bothered her. Her effort to free him enabled her to live her own life without fear or guilt — free to enter into a normal, healthy relationship with another man.

Hopefully we trust that her husband is in the Land of Light where he belongs, and where he is free to grow according to the law of the world beyond.

BELLA

Not every one was as amenable to the directions, nor were they, the earth-bound, always willing to respond to the efforts of the living. Lydia's husband, having no desire to trouble her, co-operated and left as soon as he learned how to proceed. But when in the same week another woman came to me seeking a release from her dead husband, the response was quite different. Her husband did not want to let go! He was not amenable. He had dominated his wife all the forty years of their marriage, during which times she never openly rebelled or asserted herself. In her own words she confessed, "It was easier for me to give in and I always did, but I never liked it. I deeply resented his attitude, but I kept my feelings hidden. I never really cared for him. I was relieved when he passed on".

Bella had been a faithful, obedient wife, subordinating her feelings, serving his needs albeit resentfully, and now she wanted her freedom. "But," she added, "he won't let me go. l think he is still hanging around!"

"What makes you think so?" I asked. "Your marriage was not a particularly loving one, and now that he is free to go on he may welcome the separation from you. He may be happy to go on to the world beyond".

She looked at me with a look I have often seen in the eyes of people coming for this kind of help — a look mixed with fear and hope — a fear of revealing the bizarre, and a hope that someone will understand.

She continued, "Every night I feel a tingling in my hands and feet, my whole body vibrates, and then he is there with me, talking to me the same way he did when he was alive. He is always advising me, trying to get me to do what he wants, trying to prevent me from doing what I want — just like he always did. I can't stand it! He makes me nervous. He upsets me. I don't want him bossing me around anymore!"

Obviously she wanted to be free of him and would do anything to obtain that freedom. I explained our method and she eagerly agreed to do anything in order to get rid of that unwanted presence.

We went through the familiar routine of communicating with the dead. She begged him to go away and leave her in peace. He resisted, exhibiting the same characteristic stubbornness in death as in life! He didn't want to let go. He didn't want to do anything that would weaken his domination over her. He refused to budge!

I explained to Bella something I firmly believe — that death does not change the fundamental characteristics of a person. Life is the workshop where changes, if any, take place. What we are, our essential being, we take with us when we cross the line to the other side. This stubborn, headstrong, domineering husband was still trying to control his wife from the grave, so to speak. Now she would have to be persistent and firm — something she never was able to be in the long years of her marriage.

We were in a difficult spot which required time and persistence.

Fortunately we were able to enlist the help of a daughter who loved her parents and was sympathetic to her mother's plight. Now both of them, wife and daughter, joined in pleading with the dead man to let go. He was difficult and resistent. It required great patience. But they never gave up. Each night for three weeks mother and daughter together 'prayed' and 'talked' to the deceased. The daughter was unbelievably helpful in persuading her father to give up. Reassuring him of her love for him, she urged him to leave her mother alone and go in peace. Finally, their combined persistent efforts succeeded as the tingling, vibrating sensations and the inner conversation ceased. The tormented woman was finally released from what could have been a deteriorating existence for both the living and the dead.

LAURA

There are many who experience the presence of the dead around them without fear or desire to change anything. Shortly after a great loss they find comfort in the continuing relationship, and as time goes on they become so accustomed to that other presence in their lives that it never occurs to them that such an existence is unhealthy. The more loving a relationship, the more tempting it is to encourage its continuance, long after a physical contact, as we know it, is possible.

Laura never suspected that her ready acceptance of the presence of her father, dead since she was fourteen, could have affected her long-standing marriage to Ben! Laura was five years old when she announced to her parents that when she grew up she was going "to marry daddy!" She was a beautiful child. Her father doted on her and basked in the warmth of the little girl's adoration of him. Many a daughter has felt this kind of love for her father, but few, if any, had their whims gratified in the way little Laura had her wishes come true. Without realizing the full meaning of such an act, Laura's parents thoughtlessly arranged a mock marriage ceremony! Laura decked out in a white dress with a kind of makeshift veil, walked down an aisle and became the bride of her father! Of course, the adults thought it was hilarious and thoroughly enjoyed the masquerade. To little Laura it was real. Her magnificent daddy had made her dreams come true, and her secret desire to be his bride was fulfilled. What a wonderful father! How he gave in to her every wish! How she adored him! She would love him "forever and forever!"

I am certain that none of the adults realized the damaging effects of such an action on the emotions of a little girl. And Laura was to pay the price for a very long time.

When Laura was fourteen, her father died, leaving the grief stricken young "bride" a prey to her uncontrollable emotions. At eighteen she blossomed into an exceptionally beautiful young lady, charming and lovable, but always highly emotional, at times bordering on hysteria. Just out of high school she met Ben, fell madly in love, and married him.

I didn't know her in those early years. We first met when she was in her mid-forties. At that time she was still trying to cope with her emotions and had joined a group in order to find help and understanding of the problems caused by her volatile nature. She was a beautiful woman. We became good friends — a friendship which exists to this very day. I knew her for many years before I realised the source and depth of her problem. Prior to joining the group, she had five years of psychiatry which she said helped but never got to the root cause of her troubles.

For business reasons Ben was transferred to another city, and for a few years we lost contact with each other. When they moved back again, we resumed our relationship. By this time I was deeply involved in working for the dead and had begun to talk often to the groups about the various problems connected with the effect of the dead on the lives of the living. Attending this particular meeting, Laura was noticeably excited, asked many questions and seemed anxious to probe deeper. Later she approached me and asked if we could meet as soon as possible. She had "so much to tell me!"

She was eager to reveal her innermost feelings, particularly as they related to her father. I already knew about the mock marriage that had occurred when she was five years of age, but I didn't know how deeply the memory colored her real marriage ceremony to Ben.

"You know," Laura confided, "how close Ben and I are and how much I've always loved him. There is no one like Ben and I am the luckiest woman to have such devotion, such consideration. But I have never understood why a heavy weight descended upon me the night of our marriage. I love Ben passionately, but I have always been puzzled by that overwhelming sadness which came over me from the moment he kissed me, the bride. To this very day, particularly in our bedroom, I am filled with that same incomprehensible sadness. It has never left me".

Twenty-six years of marriage, a good loving marriage marred by an unknowable intrusion. The mock marriage of the child confusing the real marriage of the adult. Was it the memory that brought on the "sadness" or was it something else? Could it be the presence of the father?

As though reading my mind Laura continued, "That is not all, I know you will understand when I tell you that often, very often, when I enter my bedroom I know that my father is there. At night when I turn over in my sleep I am often confused as to who is in the bed next to me, Ben or my father!"

No wonder Laura was overly emotional! No wonder she lacked energy! No wonder she had had so many illnesses over the years. That ever-loving shadowy presence was overwhelming her, robbing her of the joy which marriage to a man like Ben should have given her. No wonder a feeling of sadness was permeating the atmosphere. Wanting the best for his daughter, the father was unwittingly giving her the worst. She was trapped and he was trapped!

Laura was thinking of her father's plight when she asked what she could do in order to release him. She was more sensitive to his condition than her own predicament. Oblivious to the deleterious effect on herself she kept repeating, "Poor daddy. How awful for him. All these years of confinement. Can we help him?"

I gave her two choices on the procedure: either she could work with me, or else Jennifer and I could try to make the contact without her. Although I usually preferred working directly with the closest living relative, I realized that emotionally and physically Laura was in no condition to encounter her dead father. Without hesitation Laura chose that we do it for her. She admired and respected Jennifer. She trusted me.

Jennifer was out-of-town at this time, and I promised Laura that we would do the 'work' as soon as possible, but meantime she could co-operate by doing a special meditation for her father. She was given the image of a circle of light in which she placed her father, visualizing this picture every morning and every evening. I could not tell her when Jennifer and I would work as Jennifer was not certain of the date of her return to the city.

It so happened that Jennifer returned earlier than scheduled and we got together soon after. Jennifer had another special problem to work out, and when we finished we decided that there was ample time to look into Laura's case. Because neither of us had known Laura's father, I thought it would take longer and be more difficult than usual. Quite to the contrary, Laura's father came into our orbit easily and without hesitation. Heavy and sad, he was a forlorn spectacle! From the moment he 'appeared' I was aware of a pain in his throat — a pain which I felt in my own throat during the entire session.

We conversed with him by way of thought transference, which seems to be the means of communicating with the dead. The words we use are for our own benefit as the dead understand the thought behind the words. The pictures and images form a common ground for all of us. In imagery we saw that father and daughter were tied to each other at the solar plexus. The ties were strong. We conveyed to the father the message that Laura wanted us to help release him. We 'told' him that the ties which attached him to Laura were about to be cut. We assumed that he, as well as Laura, was desirous of obtaining freedom and the fact that he was present indicated that he too was willing.

As we talked the atmosphere began to lighten. With his seeming consent, we cut the ties which symbolized his and Laura's strong emotional attachment. All the time we were doing the so-called cutting-the-ties, we were reassuring him that he would no longer be a lost soul bound to his daughter's bedroom, but that he would be free to go to the glorious world beyond.

When the ties at the solar plexus were finally cut and severed, we proceeded to heal the gaping wounds by the simple method known as "laying on of hands". All of this was done in imagery. As we were doing the healing, again I became aware of the pain in his throat and almost automatically I put my hands on his throat, praying for a complete healing. The picture began to fade, the healing was over. Before leaving we told Laura's father to be sure to look for the Light that would guide him on his journey.

For the next few days neither Jennifer nor I were able to contact Laura in order to tell her what had been done. Therefore, when Laura called it was evident to me that my emotional friend had not succumbed to suggestion, but had experienced first hand the extraordinary effects of our work.

Laura's first words were triumphant. "I *know* that you and Jennifer worked for me and my father, and I *know* just what day you did it". She then proceeded to give me the exact day! When I confirmed the fact, she was delighted and continued, "I knew because that very night there was a lightness between Ben and me that was new and different, as though a heavy weight had been lifted from our very bed! Even Ben noticed the difference and when he wondered about it and made some comments, I didn't tell him what I thought must have happened. How could I? He would have found it all too difficult to believe. But I am so happy and so grateful".

Now Laura wanted to know all the details and I proceeded to

give her a complete account of what we had done. She was impressed by the significance of the tie being at the solar plexus, the so-called 'seat of the emotions' She commented that whenever she was particularly upset she always felt the reaction in that region of her body (as most emotional people do). I told her that I believed that from now on she would notice a difference in her emotional reactions and that physically she should begin to improve.

Suddenly, I recalled the great pain at her father's throat. I told Laura about it, that it had puzzled me, and that we had concluded the session with a healing treatment not only at the solar plexus but also at his throat.

For a moment there was a hushed silence, then Laura's awestruck voice. "I understand why you felt that pain in his throat but you didn't know. How could you know. I forgot to tell you. My father died of cancer of the throat!"

Though no longer skeptical, I am continuously given added evidence that our experiences with the dead are valid. I have no other way of accounting for the pain in my throat when I sensed the presence of Laura's dead father who had died of throat cancer! I have no other way of accounting for the instantaneous relief given to Laura when the tie between her and her father had been cut.

For many long years Laura had been carrying a heavy burden. Now that the weight has been lifted from her, she is experiencing a joy in living which had always eluded her. The journey through life for most people is difficult enough without adding unnecessary luggage. Laura, freed from her oppressive load is at long last able to express joyously her deep love for an adored husband.

We are convinced that Laura's father, by his very presence and co-operation, was also seeking a release. We assumed that he too was weary of struggling against the heavy obstacles blocking his way to freedom, obscuring the Light on his path.

These cases clearly demonstrated to us the kind of predicament in which many of the earth-bound dead and the living find themselves. There are many other ways in which the dead can affect the lives of the living

Bad habits, addictions to drugs and alcoholism may be caused by the obsessive influence of those who have passed on but are still earth-bound.

One such case involving alcoholics has been reported by Dr. Viola Neal.[1] A young man, Paul, who was one of her clients, came to her for help. Shortly after the death of his alcoholic brother he became addicted to the same compulsive desire for liquor. Up until this time Paul had never cared much for 'the stuff,' as he called it. Having observed over the years the disastrous effects of alcohol on his brother, Paul had an aversion and distaste for it. After his brother, highly intoxicated, died suddenly in an automobile accident, Paul became a compulsive drinker — an alcoholic. He could not pass a bar without being compelled to go in and order a few drinks. His will to resist 'the stuff' was completely destroyed. He could not understand or cope with the sudden obsession and was miserably unhappy. As the months rolled by and the obnoxious habit seriously affected his business and his family life, Paul became desperate.

After much questioning, Dr. Neal concluded that Paul's dead brother was imposing his own desire for liquor on Paul. Although the brother was dead, the overpowering desire for liquor was still there and he sought to quench his burning thirst through Paul. Dr. Neal instructed Paul in the method of talking to the dead which he immediately applied to his problem. Paul was not only accustomed to meditation, but was also a student who believed in life after death. Ater three days of meditation and engaging his brother in conversation, Paul happily reported that he had succeeded in breaking the connection between himself and his brother. The obsessive desire for liquor was gone and Paul was free — able once again to lead a normal life.

Other cases of compulsive alcoholism after death have come to my attention. Some turn to alcohol for solace in order to relieve the oppressive presence of the deceased. Others, like Paul, become victimized by the influence of an earth-bound alcoholic who uses the physical body of another in order to satisfy his own insatiable desires. Both types have been helped by the method described. Not all alcoholics, however, fall into either of the above categories. Obviously there are many other reasons for alcoholism.

The simplicity of the method, the ease by which so much is gained, usually surprises those who receive help. It is diffcult for many of them to understand how a few well-chosen words and a sincere prayer can bring about such a dramatic improvement in their lives. Those who have personally experienced the great sense of well-being and freedom which results from the release often express amazement that so little can accomplish so much. As one man summed it up, "No one can imagine the heavy weight of such a burden. It is a constant torment, a nameless sadness. It is incredible that I was relieved of so much distress and helped so easily and quickly".

More things are wrought by prayer than
this world dreams of.

Alfred Tennyson — *The Passing of Arthur*

Chapter 10

The Act of Severance

The ties to the dead are unsuspected because too few of us accept the 'livingness' of the so-called dead. If we could understand that the dead have cast off their physical body only, that everything else is still the same as it was before the demise, then we would approach the problem of our particular role from a new perspective. The need for our understanding of their condition is so important.

There is a role which the living can play if they wish to help ease the transition for the departed one. No one can, nor should, suppress grief at such a moment, but if at the same time the grief-stricken survivor can remember the needs of the one who has just "crossed the bar" and offer a comforting word, then much of the sorrow for both can be alleviated.

Many people make the transition normally and automatically. They slip into a peaceful slumber without any problem, but there are an unbelievable number who, for one reason or another, resist making the normal exit. Fear of the unknown has paralyzed them so that what should be a happy transition becomes a terrible trauma. In their fear, they close the door to a glorious experience and remain in a no-man's land of sadness and frustration. The bereaved wife, husband, mother, father, and other close relatives can render a great service to these hapless sufferers.

Conversing with them daily for at least a few weeks after the death is one way of helping them. For some reason beyond logical comprehension, the so-called dead seem to get the message. The closer the relationship, the easier is the communication. If there have been any disagreements and misunderstandings, talk about it. If there is any feeling of guilt, it is quite possible that the guilt is shared. Forgive! Ask to be forgiven! Help by releasing the dead from burdensome and binding emotions. All the while constantly reassure the lost ones and tell them to follow the Light. The Light is always there — they must be told that it is there. It is there to guide them into the land of fulfillment. The dead need our words of comfort, not our over-whelming grief. They need our understanding and knowledge of what they are experiencing, and our prayers can be directed to that need.

If all who are bereaved could engage the departed one in such a conversation, much unnecessary suffering could be eliminated. We would have fewer earth-bound souls and fewer problems caused by the earth-bound. Holding tightly to the grief, guilt, and resentments, clinging to the past with overly indulged emotions, can perpetuate the stress and encourage a continuance of an association. This is unhealthy. The dead must go on to their destination and the living must go on and finish out the schedule allotted to them at birth.

As much as one loves the departed, it is wrong to want the questionable comfort of the dead in the atmosphere of the living. The time for working out the problems in an active relationship with the deceased is over. The time for severing the tie has come.

There is a great need to understand this and put to practice the Act of Severance.

What is the Act of Severance? It is an action undertaken by the living for the purpose of freeing the dead from their bondage to anything or anyone connected with the material world. It is an act of mercy based on the assumption that the earth-bound dead are helpless and sorely in need of assistance. Usually it is more effective if it is carried out by a close relative or a devoted friend of the dead. Existing in a land of emptiness, adrift on a vast sea, rudderless with no compass, the earth-bound dead eagerly and thankfully respond to the directions given them by a caring person. The Act of Severance performed by the living cuts the ties that anchor the dead to an existence no longer viable.

The Act of Severance also benefits the living. Released from the crippling ties to the dead, the living can now actively go forward into life. Free from the debilitating burden of such a tie, the survivors are restored to mental, physical and emotional health. The living have the power and the right to perform the Act of Severance when necessary.

When and how can the Act of Severance be carried out? The following instructions are given for those who would like more precise directions.

When after the death of a loved one you feel a sense of their presence around you, then it is possible that the departed one is attached to you. If as time goes on that sense of their presence continues and makes you feel ill, sleepless, depressed, or any of the other symptoms previously described, then it is up to you to perform the Act of Severance in order to release yourself from the departed one. Remember, you are serving the dead as well as yourself.

Even if you have no sense of their presence, no disturbing manifestations (as some do), but seem unable to return to normal health, then you can begin to suspect that you are a victim. If your physical and emotional health continues to deteriorate to an alarming degree, worsening over a long period of time after the death, then you should perform the Act of Severance.

If for some personal reason you are reluctant to engage in this effort, then ask someone whom you love and trust to do it for you. It is perfectly proper to ask some close relative or friend to join you when making the contact. I have found that many people preferred the presence of another person. Others preferred to ask two sympathetic and understanding friends to make the contact for them. It doesn't seem to matter whether or not the survivor is present as long as the message is conveyed with love and under-standing. Alone, accompanied by another, or performed by two caring people, the results are the same — release from suffering and distress.

A final word of caution: If you have accomplished the release for yourself, you will be tempted to help others with a similar problem. Do not interfere unless you discuss the situation with them and ask their permission. There are some who enjoy the presence of the dead around them and would not welcome any intrusion in their private world. Never, never interfere. It is a law. Do not break it — no matter how tempted you are to help. You can harm yourself by such interference. The only exception to the rule, the only time you do not have to ask permission, is when your own child, parent, or spouse is involved. The closeness of the relationship gives you the right to help them.

Finally, whenever you feel that the time for prolonged grieving is over and the time for resuming your normal life has come, then sever the tie.

How is the Act of Severance performed? Find a quiet, comfortable place in your home — perhaps a chair in a room familiar to the dead. Choose a time when you, the server, will be reasonably certain of quiet. The time and place should be free of any chance of interruption. Having established the setting, relax. Breathe in and out rhythmically; at the same time listen to your inhalations and exhalations. With eyes closed, visualize the breath as it comes and goes from the nostrils. Tell your entire body to relax. Your favorite prayer will help. When you are reasonably relaxed, yet awake and alert, you are ready to contact the one who has passed on.

Silently or vocally call the person by name several times and establish the relationship. Now begin your conversation. Tell the person the reason for your trying to communicate. Tell the person the circumstances of the death — every detail. Very often the dead are not aware that they have passed on, and so it is important that they be told. Be very explicit.

Remain calm and don't expect answers. Explain that remaining around the earth without a physical body is destructive to both of you. If you have been unusually distressed, nervous, sleepless or ill since the demise, then say so and emphasize the fact that their presence is harming you. Reassure your loved ones that they will be looked after when they finally depart from the material world, and will benefit by the release. Last of all tell the departed to look for the guiding Light, for helpers, relatives or friends who have gone on before. Give a final word of love and blessing. If you wish, finish with the Twenty-third Psalm. Repeat if necessary the entire process several times for about three days.

Unless your symptoms both physical and emotional are from other causes, you will feel better, sometimes immediately. Sleeplessness, irritability and nervousness, unless they are old unrelated symptoms, will disappear dramatically. Fears and angers that had developed shortly after the demise will vanish as they did for Ronald, the husband of one of the students.

Shortly after the death of his father, Ronald became unduly angry and irritable. Thinking he was exhausted from the many months of watching a beloved parent dying from cancer, Ronald's wife, Ruth, assumed that he was suffering a normal fatigue resulting from the strain. It wasn't until Ronald's anger and irritability worsened and became unbearable for her and his colleagues at the office that Ruth concluded it must be her father-in-law who was producing in his son his own characteristic tendencies to great angers and irritability. When Ruth tried to tell Ronald how badly he was behaving and how it was destroying his relationships with her and others, he replied that he couldn't help it. He was unable to control his angers. Everyone would have to learn to put up with it!

Ruth had prayed for her father-in-law at the time of his funeral and thought that the usual prayer conducted at that time was suffcient. But the reactions of her husband made her aware that more had to be done. Realizing that the father, a powerful personality, had been unusually close to his son, she concluded that somehow the two were still tied. When she discovered the cause of the trouble she knew how and what to do. She wasted no time in contacting her father-in-law in the manner described above.

In spite of her knowledge and familiarity with the Act of Severance, Ruth was astonished when three hours later Ronald returned home a different man. Restored to his normal self, he opened the door with his old but recently neglected greeting, "Hi honey, I'm home. How did your day go?" Although not everyone responds as speedily as Ruth's husband, yet given a reasonable period of time, many experience the great release within a few days, or at most a few weeks.

Never take anything for granted. Any unusual behavior pattern immediately following the death of someone close, continuing for many months or years, increasing in intensity rather than diminishing, should be looked upon as a warning signal. Perhaps the departed is still earth-bound, still attached, still emotionally tied to the one closest to him. When time does not heal, then it is time to consider performing the Act of Severance.

As I have observed the effects on the living before and after the Act of Severance, I realize that the knowledge that has been given is practical. Although founded on mystical principles, the accomplishments are realistic and the results continuously give evidence that the findings are based on a workable solution.

Empty the boat of your life, O man:
when empty it will swiftly sail. When
empty of passions and harmful desires
you are bound for the land of Nirvana.

The Buddha — *Dhammapada 369*

Chapter 11

The Survivors

That there are a great number of survivors who suffer abnormally after the death of a loved one has recently been the subject of a survey conducted by Dr. J. William Worden of Harvard University. According to the report made public by *The National Enquirer*, the study found that, "The death of a husband or wife has a direct effect on the health of the surviving spouse".[1] The survey matched a group of sixty-eight persons who had lost their mates against a group of sixty-eight married persons. It was found that, "After fourteen months the bereaved group had more sick days in bed than the non-bereaved group — more hospital admissions, more sleep disturbances, and increased consumption of alcohol, tobacco and tranquilizers".[2] Emotional problems, sleeplessness and restlessness were also included in the problems of the bereaved.

Strangely and coincidentally, I came across this article just as I was in the midst of writing this chapter. Was it by chance that I was prompted to buy *The National Enquirer* and read about the Harvard University study? Originally I was motivated to write this book because of the suffering of the survivors and a desire to share with them a way of finding relief. Although I am well aware that there could be other causes for the deteriorating health of the "surviving spouse", yet I am personally convinced that there are many who are distressed by the continuing influence or presence of the departed. The survey made at Harvard University indicates that there is a problem, that the "surviving spouse" is in trouble, but the article does not make any reference to a remedy.

However, a method has been tried which seems to relieve those survivors who demonstrated that they had been affected by the de-energizing power of the earth-bound dead. There would be little value in writing a book about my personal experiences with the dead and their effect on the living if a way of helping them had not been found. Because there is a simple procedure which anyone can follow, I thought that it is important that this knowedge be shared.

For some years I mistakenly believed that it required personal direction and specific training in order to influence the dead to release their attachment to the living. Later I discovered that anyone, the person directly involved, a close relative, or a devoted friend can talk to the dead and direct them to the Light. This is why I, and others, have encouraged the survivors who have been besieged and weakened by the presence of the dead to apply the simple method as described. Talking to the dead is as easy (sometimes easier) as talking to the living! In many instances, the results are so incredible that they continuously amaze and astound me.

My involvement led me step by step into working with the problem of the earth-bound dead and their ties to the living. I am fully aware that there is a great need for more instructions on how to prevent the living from falling into a self-made trap — a trap dark with fear. Those who are obsessed with the thought of oblivion, and by the emotion of fear, usually have great difficulty in making the transition from life into death, into life in the beyond. Their fear becomes an obstruction which hides the Light and often leads the dying into the very oblivion that caused the fear in the first place. In order to escape the dark trap of fear or oblivion, the dead sometimes cling to the life form of another. Either choice is wrong and detrimental.

A knowledge of the death process and life beyond death can save anyone from falling into the trap of fear, the state of oblivion, or the unsatisfactory condition of an earth-bound soul. As Hugh L'Anson Fausset, in his book *Fruits of Silence*, has so well said, "We have been so long conditioned to regard our existence here as a fight for life, that we forget that it is not death we must and can overcome, but our dread of it".[3]

In order to enter freely into the next life beyond death, the fact must be accepted that death is not the end of existence — it is only the end of a particular physical life. The fact must be accepted that death is simply discarding the old form and taking on a new one designed to meet the conditions of the next dimension.

There are many people who cannot or will not accept this fact. Life is so precious and real to them, their families so very dear. Death is not for them, they think. It is for the other person, some one else. These same people cannot foresee a time when they will no longer be able to continue in their familiar pattern of existence. They refuse to accept the inevitable event, and when faced with a terminal disease their "fight for life" dominates every moment. It becomes their all-consuming activity.

Although it is right to "fight for life" (and one should) yet there comes a time when the truth must be faced. When the final moments come, the uninformed now approaches that period in his life which calls for a special kind of help.

Larry was a typical example of the type who refused to admit the possibility of death. He repeatedly told his wife, Cynthia, that he did not want any discussion about death. He was convinced that death was the end of everything for everyone and he did not want to talk about it. It was too dreadful!

Larry had terminal cancer. When the physician announced that it was now a "matter of a few weeks," Cynthia tried again to broach the subject in the hope of preparing Larry for the next lap on his journey. Being convinced that death is just another incident in the life process, she attempted to persuade him to her point of view. Though grief stricken, she yearned to comfort her husband by sharing with him her belief that their parting would be only temporary. But by this time Larry was too much immersed in his own pain and fear to respond.

Finally, when Larry became comatose, no longer communicative, no longer able to protest, Cynthia decided that she still had time to help him — to remind him again that death was not the end. She sat by his bedside, held him in her arms and reassured him over and over again that he was not going very far away from her and his loved ones. She kept referring to his forthcoming experience as a wonderful journey which he was about to take, and that eventually she would join him.

"Don't worry about me," she consoled, "I will miss you, but I know that we shall be together again. You will find happiness in the next stop on your journey. Look for your parents. Look for the Light. You are going to be well taken care of".

It takes great faith to converse in this way with an inert, almost lifeless human being. But Cynthia believed in what she was doing and was intent on bringing comfort to her departing husband.

On the third day of her continuous conversations, something happened which convinced Cynthia that Larry might have heard.

Cynthia and I were in the hospital bedroom conversing quietly about the possibility of her messages being understood by Larry. Suddenly as though in answer to our speculation, the lifeless form came to life! Larry, lifting his head from the pillow, eyes wide open, called out loudly and clearly, "Cynthia!" That was all. His head fell back. He returned to his comatose condition. Although she did not look for confirmation, Cynthia was now sure in her own mind that Larry had heard and had made a superhuman effort to tell her that he understood.

An intelligent and believing survivor can assist the dying as well as the dead, whose fear has prevented them from searching for the truth. Never willing to face the fact of death as part of life, Larry was frightened when the supreme moment came. Having accepted the fact that death is impossible, Cynthia was able to help him.

When the truth about death is understood, then there will be no need for the rescue work herein described. The dying will release their hold on a physical body rendered useless either by infirmities or accident, and accept the new status in the world beyond with intelligence. But until this is universally understood, the problem of the dead sometimes clinging to the living will continue and the need for the living to participate in a rescue operation will be essential.

The enlightened human being will know how to meet his own death. The enlightened human being will know how to help departed relatives and friends release themselves from the material world. The enlightened human being will know how to direct the so-called dead to the Bright Light shining on their path, leading them home, to the Source.

Much has been written and said about the Light, the Light of God — the ever present, everlasting Light on the path. It is here. It is there. It is everywhere. No one who sees It can turn away from It. All who see It yearn to unite with It. When the Self makes the journey home, the path is bright with the Light and nothing else matters! The Light is there! All is well!

This, our present cycle, is the end of
the age, and the next two hundred
years will see the abolition of death, as
we now understand that great transition, and the establishing of the fact of
the soul's existence. [4]

Alice Bailey — *Death: The Great Adventure*

Epilogue

The Teacher

The little girl in the schoolroom sees the Teacher. He is standing beside a blackboard. He has a long pointer in his hand which he uses to demonstrate the lesson. The child's attention wavers. She listens and hears the words. Mechanically she repeats what she hears — and believes that she knows.

The years pass. The child becomes the young woman. She is in an advanced class. The Teacher is still there. She hears the words. They are more complicated now, more difficult, and she repeats mechanically what she hears. She memorizes and believes she knows. The Teacher is patient. He knows that she doesn't know. He knows that she is awake only to the words, the facts, but not to the meaning. She is asleep to the meaning. She is unable to apply the facts to her life.

The mature woman falters. She has now become addicted to sleep walking, hurting herself, hurting others in her seeming blindness. The Teacher is still there, patiently waiting — waiting for the day when she will wake up.

Her rebirth is a long time in coming. The Teacher is patient. He has all eternity! He prods, hoping to awaken her. Her life is half over. The moment has come. Time is running out. She stirs. Something is wrong, or is it right? There is a blinding flash of light! The birth of meaningfulness, of joy, of wisdom, of purpose! She is awake — painfully and happily awake!

The Teacher is patient. Now his work really begins. Step by step he guides her. The path is strewn with obstacles. He teaches her the meaning, the purpose of facing the truth, the purpose that the obstacles can serve. He is there as she removes them one by one, clearing the path. He leads the way through the twists and turns of the road. He is patient. She falters. She weakens. He waits. He knows that she will never turn back, never go to sleep again. The Light of Truth is now on her path. She has reached a crossroads. Will she remain there? Will she be content to come this far and go no further?

She wants to stop. She has worked hard. She is weary. Going on means severing connections, losing the comfort of close relationships. She hesitates and considers. She meditates. She has learned to rely on the Teacher. What does He want her to do? The answer comes in a significant dream. She must go forward. She knows now that she can be obedient only to the Teacher — to Life.

One woman's story can be everyone's story. The purpose of life is lost when the protagonist is asleep, mechanically obeying the whims of others. The Great Teacher is fulfilled when His pupil wakes up.

The student tries to transmit the message to those in trouble, to other seekers. She tells them all that she knows about the Teacher. Her chief aim is to help each one find his or her inner teacher.[1] Some listen, hear what they want to hear, absorb what they are ready for. Others probe more deeply, more courageously, more trustingly. They, the persistent seekers, find the key that opens their own door which leads them into a future bright with promise. They wake up! Life begins for them. They see the pattern of their own existence. They learn to accept their deficiencies and face the truth calmly. Life becomes a great adventure in growth, in awareness, in consciousness. They too begin to understand the meaning behind the words. They know!

A total acceptance of life, a commitment to its teachings, leads the student step by step to a deeper understanding of the culminating event — death into life. Life is revealed in its wholeness — the full cycle of birth, life, death — all one.

The Great Teacher is always within us. It is Life — everlasting.

Death is only an interlude in a life of steadily accumulating experience... it marks a definite transition from one state of consciousness into another.

Alice Bailey — *From Bethlehem to Calvary* [2]

Notes

Introduction   New Edition

1. Sogyal Rinpoche, *The Tibetan Book of Living and Dying*, Harper San Francisco, 1992
2. Elisabeth Kübler-Ross, *On Death and Dying*, Scribner, New York, 1969; *Death the Final Stage of Growth*, Prentice-Hall International 1975; *On Life After Death*, Celestial Arts, Berkeley, CA, 1991
3. Raymond Moody, *Life after Life*, Bantam Books, 1975
4. Robert Whitaker, *Anatomy of an Epidemic*, Broadway Books, New York, 2015
5. Edward Tick, *War and the Soul: Healing Our Nations Veterans from Post-Traumatic Disorder*, Quest Books, Wheaton, Ill. 2005, p. 138
6. Andrew Powell, *The Ways of the Soul. A Psychiatrist Reflects: Essays on Life, Death and Beyond*. Muswell Hill Press 2017, pp.161-2
7. Anita Moorjani *Dying to be Me*, Hay House Inc., New York, 2012
8. Penny Sartori and Kelly Walsh, *The Transformative Power of Near-Death Experiences*, Watkins, London 2017
9. Account of Victor Solov, Marie-Louise von Franz, *On Dreams and Death*, Shambhalla, Boston & London, 1986, p. 147
10. Randall, *The Supreme Adventure*, James Clarke & Co. Ltd., 1961.1974, p. 11

Chapter 1   The Dream of Liberation

1. A tried and tested way of working for transpersonal psychotherapists. Barbara Somers and Ian Gordon-Brown, *Journey in Depth: A Transpersonal Perspective*, Archive Publishing: Shaftesbury: 2002, p.176, 213, 226
2. Barabara Somers and Ian Gordon-Brown, *Symptom as Symbol: A Transpersonal Language*, Archive Publishing, Shaftesbury: 2010, p.226

Chapter 2   **The Moon People**

1. Recommended reading: Barbara Somers and Ian Gordon-Brown, *Journey in Depth: A Transpersonal Perspective*, Archive Publishing: Shaftesbury: 2002, p.237-254
2. Jung's 'active imagination' is the basis of 'guided imaging' in the transpersonal perspective. Barbara Somers and Ian Gordon-Brown, *The Raincloud of Knowable Things: a Practical Guide to Transpersonal Psychology*, Archive Publishing: Shaftesbury: 2008, p.253-266
3. Part of a quotation from the 'Emerald Tablet' of Hermes Trismegistus from the Alchemical tradition. *The Fires of Alchemy, A Transpersonal Viewpoint*, Archive Publishing: Shaftesbury: 2004, p.156, xxiv (appendix II)

Chapter 5   **Release and Freedom**

1. Phyllis Krystal was a British Psychotherapist who lived and practiced for many years in California. Author of several books on guided imagery and visualisation techniques. Probably the best known is *Cutting the Ties That Bind*, Turnstone Press, Wellingborough: 1982. Samuel Weiser: Maine: 1993. All have been reprinted.
2. ibid, p. 75-76

Chapter 7   **Jim Senior and Jim Junior**

1. Another reference to Phyllis Krystal's work using the 'figure of eight' which can be found in *Cutting the Ties That Bind*, and *Cutting More Ties That Bind*.

Chapter 9   **The Earth-Bound**

1. Dr Viola Pettit-Neal, *Through the Curtain*, DeVorss & Co: California: 1983

Chapter 10   **The Survivors**

1. Dr. J. William Worden, *The National Enquirer*, published article of results of survey.
2. Dr. J. William Worden, *Grief Counseling and Grief Therapy*, Springer: New York: 1982 (Several Editions)
3. Hugh l'Anson Fausset, *Fruits of Silence: Studies in the Art of Being*, Abelard-Schuman: New York: 1963 (Now part of HarperCollins)
4. Alice Bailey, "Death: The Great Adventure", *A Treatise on the Seven Rays*, The Lucis Trust: London: 1936

Epilogue   **The Teacher**

1. The inner Teacher has been known by various names: Spirit, Soul, Higher Self or Atman. Jung called it the Self, whose wisdom becomes accessible to us once we awaken to Its Presence.
2. Alice Bailey, *From Bethlehem to Calvary*, Lucis Trust: London: 1937

Resources

There are now many books on the Afterlife. It would be helpful for those interested to read a book like Stafford Betty's *The Afterlife Unveiled* [1] which, through seven separate accounts, gives a very clear description of different aspects of that life and how the opportunities for further growth and expansion are almost infinite.

Another very helpful book mentioned in Stafford Betty's book is *Testimony of Light* [2] by Helen Greaves, who recorded the communications from her close friend Frances Banks after her death from cancer. Betty writes that his students have told him that "this book is the most important book they ever read because it tells them not just what to expect when they die but, more importantly, *what the purpose of life is here and now.*" [3] A third book mentioned in Betty's work, first published in 1954 and reprinted many times, is *Life in the World Unseen* by Robert Benson, a Catholic priest who discovered that many of the beliefs he had absorbed through his faith were not corroborated in that other world. He communicated his discoveries and enlightening experiences to a clairaudient medium, Anthony Borgia,[4] who died in 1989.

For those interested in reincarnation, there is an excellent book called *Lifecycles: Reincarnation and the Web of Life* by Christopher Bache.[5]

Ian Pretyman Stevenson (October 31, 1918 – February 8, 2007) was a Canadian-born U.S. psychiatrist. He worked for the University of Virginia School of Medicine for fifty years, as chair of the department of psychiatry from 1957 to 1967, Carlson Professor of

Psychiatry from 1967 to 2001, and Research Professor of Psychiatry from 2002 until his death. In his lifetime he wrote several books and papers which are of interest.

Michael Newton (9 December 1931 – 22 September 2016), was a hypnotherapist who claimed to have developed his own age regression technique. He wrote *Destiny of Souls* and *Journey of Souls* amongst others as a result of documenting the results of his clinical work in spiritual hypnotherapy. These are presented in a form of case studies and Newton asserts that they uncover the hidden aspects of the spirit world.

Coming right up to date there is an exceptional book written by Andrew Powell [6] titled *Conversations with the Soul, A Psychiatrist Reflects: Essays on Life, Death and Beyond*. With a foreword by Anne Baring it includes some very interesting chapters with lots of case histories.

A recent discussion moderated by John Cleese (of *Monty Python* fame) *Is there Life after Death?*, includes The University of Virginia's Division of Perceptual Studies at the 2018 Tom Tom Festival — well worth a watch:
https://www.youtube.com/watch?v=4RGizqsLumo&t=169s

An excellent and informative website is www.victorzammit.com

As is Spirit Release Forum — http://www.spiritrelease.org/

1. Stafford Betty, *The Afterlife Unveiled*, O-Books, Winchester UK and Washington USA, 2011
2. Helen Greaves *Testimony of Light*, Originally published in 1969, republished by Rider in 2005
3. Penny Sartori and Kelly Walsh, *The Transformative Power of Near-Death Experiences*, Watkins, London 2017
4. Anthony Borgia, *Life in the World Unseen: A Detailed Description of the Afterlife*. Two Worlds Publishing Co. Ltd., London 1997
5. Christopher Bache, *Lifecycles: Reincarnation and the Web of Life*, Paragon House, New edition 1994
6. Andrew Powell, *Conversations with the Soul, A Psychiatrist Reflects: Essays on Life, Death and Beyond*, Muswell Hill Press, London 2018

www.ingramcontent.com/pod-product-compliance
Lightning Source LLC
Chambersburg PA
CBHW021111090426
42738CB00006B/604

* 9 7 8 1 9 0 6 2 8 9 4 9 2 *